THE COMPLETE GUIDE TO

INDIANA
STATE PARKS

QUARRY BOOKS

AN IMPRINT OF
INDIANA UNIVERSITY PRESS

THE COMPLETE GUIDE TO

INDIANA
STATE PARKS

NATHAN D. STRANGE

Photographs by MATT WILLIAMS

This book is a publication of

Quarry Books
an imprint of
Indiana University Press
Office of Scholarly Publishing
Herman B Wells Library 350
1320 East 10th Street
Bloomington, Indiana 47405 USA
iupress.indiana.edu

The paper used in this publication meets the minimum requirements
of the American National Standard for Information Sciences—
Permanence of Paper for Printed Library Materials,
ANSI Z39.48–1992.

This book is printed on acid-free paper.

Manufactured in China

Library of Congress Cataloging-in-Publication Data

Names: Strange, Nathan D., author. |
Williams, Matt (Photographer) photographer.
Title: The complete guide to Indiana State Parks / Nathan
D. Strange ; photographs by Matt Williams.
Description: 1st edition. | Bloomington, Indiana : Quarry
Books, an imprint of Indiana University Press, [2018]
Identifiers: LCCN 2017020637 (print) | LCCN 2017019266 (ebook) |
ISBN 9780253031518 (e-book) | ISBN 9780253025197 (pbk.)
Subjects: LCSH: Parks—Indiana—History. | Indiana—
Description and travel. | Indiana—History, Local.
Classification: LCC F527 (print) |
LCC F527 .S86 2017 (ebook) | DDC 977.2—dc23
LC record available at https://lccn.loc.gov/2017020637

4 5 6 7 8   26 25 24 23 22

This book is dedicated to the people of Indiana, visitors, employees, and volunteers who strive to maintain these inherited natural lands and public spaces, first given to the people of Indiana as a gift for generations to cherish forever. Many people have dedicated their lives to the preservation of these parks, and it has been a great honor to work with the people that see the importance of not only saving natural resources and historic locations but also the archives from which much of the research for this book was derived.

"Along the quiet trails through these reservations, it is to be expected that the average citizen will find release from the tension of his overcrowded daily existence; that the contact with nature will refocus with a clearer lens his perspective on life's values and that he may here take counsel with himself to the end that his strength and confidence are renewed."

—INSCRIBED ON THE ORIGINAL STATE PARK MAPS

CONTENTS

PREFACE

While other states might rival the size of Indiana's state park system, one thing is for sure—Indiana prides itself not on the number of parks it operates but by the quality in which each one is preserved. While currently home to 24 state parks, each offers a unique perspective on the state's history and diverse environmental antiquity. Spread across 23 counties, these lands represent the very best parts of the state, held safe from urban development and set aside for recreation and to educate the public about the natural world.

This book is a culmination of investigative research from Indiana's extensive collection of historical records and archives from public libraries, the historic Working Men's Institute Museum and Library in New Harmony, Indiana, and the Indiana State Library in Indianapolis, as well as information collected from visiting all 24 Indiana State Parks. After traveling over 5,200 miles to experience every single one of Indiana's state parks, I discovered more than an outlet for outdoor exploration. The state of Indiana and its treasured parks are rich and diverse with fascinating history, stunning landscapes, irreplaceable artifacts, historic buildings, distinctive architecture, and people proud to call themselves Hoosiers.

Indiana is a place full of various types of people from all walks of life. Connected to four different states and made up of three unique regions, the state has roughly 550 square miles of water running through its sandy glaciated north, crossing fertile rolling plains of its central cities, and cutting through the gorges of its hilly, southern expanse. Home to over 6,570,902 people, the once unspoiled state owes its legacy to the Native Americans who once ruled the land, and for whom the state is aptly named Indiana: Land of the Indians. Stretching 36,420 square miles, the state of Indiana holds a wealth of natural wonders, preserved for everyone to enjoy—now and in the future.

The purpose of this book is to offer an in-depth overview of the history, location, trails and activities, and amenities of each one of Indiana's 24 state parks. Each chapter will begin with a history of landownership, the individuals responsible for the park's creation, the staff that was involved, and unique stories that make each park special. Information about the park's location will be described, along with geological and environmental information highlighting the unique sights that make each park biologically diverse. Other activities offered will be listed in a brief explanation, as well as any special amenities offered by each park, such as a lodge or cabins—including a history of the buildings and people for who they are named. Since this is a book primarily focusing on the 100-year history of Indiana's state parks, the approach will be to start at the beginning in 1916, with each chapter moving forward in time to present day.

"Our parks and preserves are not mere picnicking places. They are rich storehouses of memories and reveries. They are guides and counsels to the weary and faltering spirit. They are bearers of wonderful tales to they who will listen; a solace to the aged and an inspiration to the young."

—RICHARD LIEBER

INTRODUCTION

THE HISTORY OF INDIANA AS A STATE

Known as "The Crossroads of America," the Hoosier state has a long history of transitory settlement and usage of the land's natural resources, as early Native Americans first used the lakes, streams, and forests for hunting, farming, and trade. Deeply connected to the world around them, the Native cultures of the Iroquois and Algonquian groups prospered from the land for thousands of years before Europeans arrived around the late 1600s. These Native groups, which included the Delaware, Potawatomi, Kickapoo, Shawnee, and Miami tribes, embraced European tools and trade but refused to give up the land they had used for centuries, and by the early 1800s all of Indiana's Native American tribes had vanished either by disease, war, or forced removal.

French explorers first entered what would become Indiana sometime around 1679, reaching South Bend and the Saint Joseph River. French Canadian fur traders followed the route and, over the course of the next few decades, dedicated trade routes were cut through the Indiana landscape. Official settlement had begun. By 1787 the US government defined present-day Indiana as part of a much larger Northwest Territory. When Ohio separated in 1800, the remaining land was renamed the Indiana Territory with Indiana meaning "Land of the Indians." The population of Native tribes in the area was so vast that the territory became the frontline for many legendary battles between migrating immigrants and Native Americans. The largest immigrant groups to settle in Indiana were German, as well as numerous immigrants from Ireland and England.

Indiana's statehood was first petitioned in 1811 by Jonathan Jennings, but due to the famed War of 1812, the plan was delayed for several years. In 1816, Jennings petitioned Congress for an enabling act, a legal procedure territories followed to begin the process of becoming a state. This act required the state's boundaries to be set and for territory leaders to meet in order to write a state constitution. During the summer of the same year, 43 delegates met at the Harrison County courthouse in Corydon, Indiana, to pen the state's constitution and create the three different parts of the state's government: the Indiana General Assembly that made the laws, the governor who saw that laws were followed, and the supreme court to decide if laws were fair. After the state constitution was written, an election was held to determine the Indiana General Assembly, and Jonathan Jennings was appointed Indiana's first governor. On December 11, 1816, Indiana was officially admitted to the United States as the 19th state of the union.

As people began to move into the newly formed state, Indiana's first state capitol in Corydon was no longer centrally located to the population. Indiana's General Assembly met to discuss the topic, and a new location where Fall Creek and the White River met in the center of the state was accepted in 1821, named Indianapolis (*polis* being Greek for city). While Indiana lacked a dependable road system for many years after accepting its new state capital, the National Road, funded by the US Congress, finally reached Indiana in 1829. Covered with a thick layer of gravel, the new road system connected Indiana's east and west borders to its neighboring states, linking Richmond, Indiana, to Terre Haute, Indiana, while running directly through Indianapolis. With the rise of travel and commerce, railroads began to be built throughout Indiana in 1847, with the first rail line running from Indianapolis to Madison. With most of the roads and rail lines being built to run through Indianapolis, the city quickly became the center of transportation and the largest city in the state. While mules were traditionally used to pull rail cars, 173 electric railways operated throughout Indiana by 1893.

Historically known as the "Hoosier" state, it is widely speculated how the term came to define the people of Indiana. According to state historian Hubert H. Hawkins, the word "Hoosier" has been widely used by the general population since the 1830s, yet no one really knows how the term was officially started. Governor Joseph Wright once stated that the term was derived from an Indian word "hoosa" meaning corn and that

Indiana boatmen transporting corn down the Mississippi were known as "hoosa men." Another story tells of a contractor named Hoosier and his "Hoosier men" working on the Louisville and Portland Canal. In a third story, Indiana rivermen were historically known to quiet down all who would attempt to fight them, giving them the name "hushers" and eventually Hoosiers. Historian Jacob P. Dunn's take on the history of the word "Hoosier" explains that the word was used to describe early pioneers in Indiana that had a certain rough and uncouth demeanor. After winning a fight with a stranger, an unnamed German resident of Clarksville was said to have raised his fists and shouted, "I am a Hussar," when asked who he was, leading many to use a similar wording as a sort of battle cry. In another story, Indiana boys flat boating down the Ohio were known to jump in the air and tap their heels together shouting "Huzza," giving them the name of "Huzza Boys." Lastly, the French called the area southeast of Vincennes, Indiana, "houshier" country, which was meant to describe the area as a bushy or brushy place. While not much is known about the true origin of the term, historical records have it spelled as either "Hooshier" or "Hoosier." No matter the term's true origin, the word has grown into a term of endearment and is worn as a badge of honor by the proud people who call Indiana their home.

GROWING POPULARITY OF OUTDOOR RECREATION
Before the days of air conditioning and television, it wasn't uncommon for thousands of people to escape the heat of the summer by going to a popular recreation area for a walk or to swim. Places such as Charlestown State Park grew from generations of people using the land for the same activities we do today. As long as humans have walked the earth, we have hiked over rugged terrain and have recognized the importance of reflecting on the landscape. As social interest connected with the preservation of land for the National Park Service, interest also grew locally toward the land in our own backyards that also needed protection. The state park system of every state grew from a national interest in preservation, conservation, and adventure.

EARLY INTEREST IN LAND PRESERVATION
While no official inventory of Indiana's forests exists prior to the middle of the 1900s, historical accounts by the state's citizens and the Government Land Office speculate that the state was 85 percent forest

only 200 years ago. Since the moderately flat forests were deemed the best locations for growing crops, half of the state's trees were cleared for farming or timber products by 1860. With 1.5 million acres of forested land left, Indiana was the leading producer of timber products in the nation by the 1900s. Today, Indiana has over 4 million acres of forest, which is only 20 percent of the state, with most of the forests located in the southern region.

If not for government-funded research that led to efficient milling and timber manufacturing techniques, it is possible Indiana would have largely clear-cut most of the state. Since helping sustain a dwindling hardwood industry was an important issue, several developments came to light that positively affected the recovery of Indiana's forests. The Organic Administration Act of 1897 played a huge part in the formation of many national forests. The new law stated that no national forest could be established unless it was set aside to protect the forest, protect the area's water conditions, or furnish a continuous supply of timber sustainably. Resolution to the act in 1898 gave tax adjustments for properties maintained as forests, and the following year "An Act for the Encouragement of Forestry" gave landowners refined tax breaks if they agreed to cut no more than 20 percent of their trees, plant a tree for every tree cut, and limit grazing by livestock within the forests. Congress began initiating many more laws to protect natural areas, such as the Weeks Act of 1911 in response to a growing erosion problem due to deforestation. As government agencies began to increase their focus on land preservation, people began to see that trees and other natural resources were not in an endless abundance. Indiana was entering an era much like the rest of the nation, where the culture was evolving away from nature being purely a commodity and instead having intrinsic personal value.

RICHARD LIEBER

After emigrating from Germany as a young man, Richard Lieber initially made Indianapolis his home. Well-known as an intense hard worker with a degree in liberal arts, he first helped start a chemical company but chose to leave the business, frustrated and having witnessed three devastating building fires. He next chose work as a journalist for two Indianapolis newspapers, working as an art and music critic before eventually becoming editor. Wishing to better himself and his career, he left the newspaper business to become a manager of a bottling company and ultimately found himself working with city government. Now in a position to really make a difference, his experience with the devastating fire led him to advocate for improved fire protection within the city of Indianapolis while also campaigning for general government reform. After years of dedication, Lieber was appointed military secretary to the governor and given the rank of colonel—forever known as Col. Richard Lieber.

Having no real interest in the outdoors, a trip in 1904 in the western United States sparked his interest in conservation. At the age of 35, Lieber traveled with two friends to Lewiston, Idaho, on a hunting expedition lasting 45 days, in which the three men and four guides traveled by foot, hunted for food, and slept out under the stars. The wildness of the Bitterroot Mountains changed his perception of the natural world, and Lieber was from then on a champion for protecting the outdoors. After returning to his home state, Lieber affirmed that Indiana held just as much splendor as the west and contained exquisiteness that could contend with any other area in the nation. After staying in a cabin in 1910, near what would become Brown County State Park, his appreciation for the treasures the state had to offer increased, saying, "This whole county ought to be bought up by the state and made into a state park so that all of the people of Indiana could enjoy this beautiful spot." The following year Lieber purchased land in the county and built a vacation home he aptly called Whip-poor-will Hollow.

As others began to discuss the idea of building state and national parks across the country, no one acted on creating a state park in Indiana until Lieber took the task upon himself and got the ball rolling—advocating for the conservation of lands to preserve natural and cultural resources.

THE EVOLUTION OF INDIANA'S STATE PARKS

After years of gaining strong political support and funding, the state park proposal began to flourish with the idea of building a public place as a gift to the people of Indiana to celebrate the state of Indiana's hundredth birthday in 1916. Serving as chairman of the local board of governors for the Fourth National Conservation Conference held in Indianapolis, Lieber was able to discuss the celebration of the state's centennial with Governor Samuel M. Ralston, and as a result Lieber was invited to serve as chairman of the committee Indiana State Centennial

Memorial of the Indiana Historical Commission. The committee was formed for the sole purpose of creating the foundation of what would become Indiana's state park system. During the centennial year, it was hoped that scenic and historical tracts of land could be secured and purchased with financial help from private citizens with subscriptions to a private fund. With funding occurring almost immediately, several locations were considered, many of which eventually became state parks, yet the rugged canyons of McCormick's Creek were chosen by happenstance as the location for Indiana's first state park. The purchase of Turkey Run occurred soon after, and the state parks system was well on its way to reaching a monumental goal in its first year.

Quickly becoming a well-known figure in the conservation movement, Richard Lieber was hired as the director of Indiana State Parks before being appointed to the director position for the Indiana Department of Conservation from 1917–1933. During his service, Lieber led a nationwide movement to establish state park systems and set a standard of quality and leadership rarely seen today.

After retiring from the Department of Conservation, Lieber continued to stay involved with the state and national parks' movement, traveling across the country to share his experiences from Indiana. While staying at the Canyon Inn at McCormick's Creek State Park, Richard Lieber passed away in 1944 at the age of 74. Shortly before his death, Lieber published the book, *America's Natural Wealth*. Within the text, Lieber outlined the central elements for growing a state park into something that would be upheld for generations, including a list of the key features he believed were central to the development of any state park trust. The gift and legacy that Richard Lieber left behind for the state of Indiana have made him forever known as the father of Indiana's state parks and a highly respected conservationist.

ENVIRONMENTAL EDUCATION

As a pioneer in environmental interpretation, today Indiana is recognized as a leader in the field of environmental education since 1923, when Indianapolis-based artist Lucy Pitschler, known as the "little lady in tennis shoes," first began enthralling visitors with knowledge and appreciation of the natural world voluntarily at McCormick's Creek, Indiana's first state park. When Richard Lieber first set out to begin the state park movement, his leading principle was to have a nature guide program in every park. His vision eventually succeeded when the Department of Conservation began seasonally funding nature guides for the first time in 1927 in McCormick's Creek, Turkey Run, and Clifty Falls. Indiana Dunes and Shakamak State Parks hired summer interpreters in 1931, and just 10 years later eight parks offered interpretive programs. By 1974, 6 full-time naturalists and 13 seasonal naturalists were hired at the same time the division hired its first full-time chief naturalist. By 2005 the number of full-time interpretive naturalists had grown to 19, with almost 50 seasonal interpretive naturalists hired for the summer. Today the state has successfully fulfilled Lieber's dream of enhancing the outdoor experience through interpretation and environmental education for park visitors, with close to 23 full-time environmental educators serving at almost every property in the state park system—with all of Indiana's state parks offering some form of summer seasonal outdoor programs. The continuous presence of environmental interpretation is also reflected not only in programs, but also in the decades of inventories of flora and fauna housed by the state park system. Not only do these parks serve as places of recreation and learning for the public, but after 100 years of collection and preservation Indiana's parks also serve as museums for the state's natural and cultural history. Since the beginning, park naturalists have been responsible for keeping records of the park's natural history. Extensive lists of plants and animals have been kept and updated, dating back to the 1930s, providing invaluable information on changes over time. Today, park employees use this information to determine strategies for natural resources management. Today's interpretive naturalists still lead the nature-based walks first started by Lucy Pitschler, while also directing interpretive centers, writing articles, creating exhibits and brochures, and developing land management plans. They remain the face and spirit of the state park system.

THE NEW DEAL

In response to the Great Depression, a political realignment began to occur in the US government, making the Democratic Party a majority and allowing for a series of social liberal programs to be created under the title the New Deal. Laws passed by both Congress and Franklin D. Roosevelt during his first term allowed for programs to develop that would address what historians refer to as the three Rs: relief from poverty and for the unemployed, recovery of the economy, and reform of the financial system to prevent a depression from happening again. The New Deal occurred in two phases, the First New Deal (1933–1934) and the Second New Deal (1935–1938). The first phase focused on dealing with the pressing bank crisis with assistance from the Emergency Banking Act and the 1933 Banking Act, and provided $500 million for relief operations through the Federal Emergency Relief Administration. It also created organizations like the Civilian Conservation Corps. The second and more controversial phase promoted labor unions, defined fair maximum working hours and a minimum wage, and issued the Social Security Act and the Fair Labor Standards Act of 1938—while also initiating a second major public works project known as the Works Progress Administration.

THE CIVILIAN CONSERVATION CORPS

Like many parks across the nation, the Civilian Conservation Corps (CCC) played an incredible role in the building of roads, shelters, restrooms, gatehouses, and bridges still in use today. During a time when the economy was struggling through economic collapse during the Great Depression, the CCC provided much-needed employment, income, and job training to men aged 18 to 23. Organized by the army, the government organization was responsible for providing the CCC food, housing, medical attention, recreation, education, and pay. Military officers supervised the companies, and as is a standard practice in army camps, reveille played in the morning and taps was played at night. In the height of the CCC's involvement, as many as 64,000 Hoosiers were hired to work and live in camps on park properties, building needed infrastructure and the basic facilities the parks would need to operate. With five dollars in their pockets and the remaining 25 dollars of their pay sent directly to their families, the men also received classroom instruction on mechanical drawing, typing, foreign languages, and art, which transferred over to their daily work as they built stunning, beautiful structures that perfectly fit into the natural landscape. The rustic artistry and design of the many buildings, stone fences, and shelters still standing decades later continue to serve as focal points to many of Indiana's state parks. The use of local materials unique to each region was intensely practiced as limestone was brought from local quarries in the southern parks, and granite boulders were used in the northern projects. Much like the park system itself, these special structures continue to stand the test of time and remain important historical pieces of the landscape.

Indiana's dedication to the CCC project created 56 CCC companies altogether, eight of which were entirely African American. Although the CCC was designed to prohibit discrimination, segregation still occurred due to the racial attitudes of the day. Despite the segregation of men by race, Indiana's Company 517 was the largest and most enduring of all of the African American CCC companies, with 250 strong-willed men. Due to their strength in numbers and veracious work ethic, Company 517 is noted as doing an amazing amount of prolific work throughout southern Indiana, especially in Fort Harrison State Park and O'Bannon Woods State Park before moving north to South Bend.

THE WORKS PROGRESS ADMINISTRATION

The Works Progress Administration, later renamed the Work Projects Administration (WPA), was the largest and most ambitious New Deal Agency and took over the CCC. At its peak, the WPA provided jobs for three million unemployed men and women, as well as many youth through the Youth National Administration. Much like the CCC, the WPA constructed buildings, built roads, and aided in many similar ways as the CCC to establish the foundation of Indiana's state parks. While government assistance was available to the poor, working for the WPA project was preferred, since it helped maintain an individual self-respect and keep an individual's trade skills proficient by providing a full-time job and an honest means for providing for one's family. Over the course of eight years, the WPA projects created millions of jobs, improving infrastructure within its first few years, before evolving into an agricultural-based program and eventually a defense program with the start of World War II. Unlike the CCC, which was mostly a military organization, the WPA also focused a great deal on art, music, theatre, and writing, employing a large number of musicians, artists, writers, actors, and directors in large arts, drama, media, and literacy projects.

STATE PARK ARCHITECTURE AND DESIGN

The creation of the CCC during the Great Depression led to a boom in construction throughout the newly established parks, including structures, hiking trails, and landscaping. In order to properly manage the work, architects and engineers were assigned to CCC camps as foremen and supervisors, while landscape architects worked out of Indianapolis designing master plans for each park. During the formidable era of state park construction, Richard E. Bishop became one of the influential architects of the time, designing many of the state park inns while working for the architectural firm Bishop, Knowlton and Carson based out of Indianapolis. Park design at the time of the state parks initial construction was influenced by the Prairie School style. This technique emphasized the use of native plants and materials, with a design intended to blend structures into the environment. The artistic philosophy chosen was designed to be representative of the inns and buildings of the time period. Native, sedimentary sandstone and limestone, as well as igneous rock, for example, were quarried on park property to build the historic structures, such as Turkey Run Inn at Turkey Run State Park, Spring Mill Inn at Spring Mill State Park, the Abe Martin Lodge at McCormick's Creek State Park, Clifty Inn at Clifty Falls State Park, and Potawatomi Inn at Pokagon State Park. West-central Indiana was at one time nationally renowned for its clay products, and during the late 1800s and early 1900s the area was famed for having dozens of factories making clay bricks used in the original construction of Turkey Run Inn.

NORTH, CENTRAL, AND SOUTH REGIONS

The initial goal of Indiana's state parks was to give Hoosiers a place where they could experience the land as it was prior to settlement. A secondary goal was to have a state park within a one-hour drive of every Hoosier. With both goals met, Indiana is now home to an incredible collection of preserved mature forests, wetlands, prairies, lakeshores, and fossil beds set aside for everyone to enjoy. The state park system is representative of Indiana's diverse landscape types and distinctive landforms covering what is best described as the north, central, and south regions. Within each region a truly unique landscape exists, and since most of the parks were established for their scenic or historic importance, they are unevenly distributed throughout the state, with some parks just a half-hour drive from one another.

The northern part of the state is distinguished by many lakes and the shoreline of Lake Michigan, as well as the maritime commerce that made the area an industrial hub. The natural landforms of the north region are a result of glacier activity, resulting in topography ranging from nearly flat to rolling hills. From sand dunes and wetlands to abundant lakes, the 45-mile shoreline of Lake Michigan contributes to the area being the coldest in the state. The added influence of cold weather makes the northern parks much more suited for winter sports than parks further south. The central part of the state has historically been largely agricultural farmland, known for fields of corn and soybeans reaching to the horizon. The parks that are in this area are either of historical or cultural value or closely tied to the historical activities of Indianapolis and other smaller cities. Largely flat, the central region contains many of the state's major population centers and was the last region to have parks added in order to supplement park visitor drive time. The region's major physical features are its large collection of streams, which are widely used for recreational purposes. The more varied topography of the southern part of the state with its steep woodland knobs has drawn more attention to the development of these parks and their outdoor activities such as hiking—with some of the largest parks in the state existing in the south. Created from weathering stream erosion and mass land movement, the landscape is some of the most diverse in the state, varying from lowlands with steep hillsides to westward sloping plains, scattered with constantly changing karst topography containing numerous sinkholes, rugged terrains, and flat-topped ridges. Southern Indiana is the state's best known region to find hills and forests and is also the area of earliest settlement near the famed Ohio River and its sprawling tributaries. The least populated area of all three regions, due to accessibility and the challenging landscape, the area has historically been best used for industry, such as oil drilling, coal mining, and limestone quarries. After visiting every single state park Indiana has to offer, these three highly diverse topographic regions appropriately characterize the entire bionetwork of the state of Indiana—ranging from sandy knobstone hills to flat river bottoms and sandy shorelines.

PROTECTION AND PRESERVATION

While the state parks were originally created to protect the special, scenic, and historical areas of the state, public use and enjoyment have also been factors that have had to be continually reviewed. Finding a fine balance between recreation and preservation has been a challenge from the very beginning, and as resources become scarcer and overrun by an increasing population, the definition of protection and preservation as applied to parks and their resources is in a constant state of evolution. With the adoption of the term "Leave No Trace" by a new era of outdoor enthusiasts, the interference of the natural landscape by park staff and guests is constantly questioned. While the landscape is always in a constant shift due to environmental impacts beyond our control, several techniques have been adopted by Indiana's state park system to ensure a balance between user experience and land preservation. When developing parks it has been a constant belief to leave at least 50 percent of the parks property undeveloped in order to maintain the ecological value of the park. Rules and regulations restricting certain types of behavior, such as gathering wood, picking wildflowers, and avoiding contact with wildlife, have been issued in order to continue a separation between the interaction of humans and the natural world. Areas deemed to have unusual scientific interest have been designated as state nature preserves in order to add additional protection to endangered species of plants and animals. Lastly, environmental education programs are present in every Indiana State Park in order to educate the public about the state's natural resources and natural processes, providing a lasting measure of protection to each state park. Special cases have been given to these rules in order to heighten visitor experience and allow guests to see the natural world in the most comfortable and accessible way possible. High vistas at most parks have been cleared of trees and overgrowth, lakes are routinely stocked with fish, and water quality management programs, such as dredging, occur in order to maintain the resources for public use. While structures such as man-made lakes and impoundments are not natural, they are added to enhance the recreational quality of the property and eventually establish a new natural ecosystem. Since each park is different, depending on its point of region and defining environment, each park property has a master plan that is routinely updated in order to properly maintain its natural resources based on the most up-to-date scientific research.

DECOMMISSIONED INDIANA STATE PARKS

Since the state park system first developed over 100 years ago, many of the properties owned and managed by Indiana's Department of Natural Resources have changed. As funding for recreational facilities and state-owned properties has made a swift decline since first being established, a few parks have been forced to fall by the wayside. While they are no longer officially state parks, the decommissioned parks properties are still used as public recreational land. Given a new name and a new entity to manage the property, many of the old park properties are now managed by the county or city in which they reside.

Muscatatuck Park became Indiana's fourth state park in 1921, located along the Muscatatuck River. Once known as Vinegar Mills, the property began when the residents of Jennings County purchased 100 acres and gave it to the state to manage as a state park. While any historic settlement structures had long decayed beyond repair, one large brick building that remained was converted into the Muscatatuck Inn. For almost 15 years the property remained virtually undeveloped and rustic. Eventually doubling in size, serious development to the property first took shape in 1936 when the WPA was assigned an extensive development project to build the main road and the park's recreational shelter buildings. As the Muscatatuck Inn became renowned for its food and as a place to take a Sunday drive, cabins were constructed to accommodate overnight visitors. A quail breeding facility was set up on the property in 1953, with a game farm raising birds for conservation clubs operating until 1962. As part of the governor's youth rehabilitation program, the property also served as a youth camp for troubled teens during the summers. Despite the fact that the park was a beautiful piece of property and overwhelmingly popular, its size compared to other state parks in the system led it to change hands in 1967. Today, the park is considered a county park and managed by Jennings County.

Bass Lake State Beach was created along a large body of water once known by early Native Americans as Winchetonqua or Beautiful Waters. Located in northern Indiana, the property was originally purchased by area citizens in order to preserve the tract of land from encroaching development. With seven acres acquired along the southwestern shore of what was already named Bass Lake, the property was given to the Department of Conservation in 1931. After the state constructed a beach using sand from the bottom of the lake, the park began to boom with popularity, eventually growing to 21 acres with the addition of a campground. Located very close to Tippecanoe River State Park, Bass Lake was co-managed by the same staff from 1971 until it was decommissioned as a state park in 2002. The property was handed over to Stark County and became a county park, due its size and continual budget cuts.

In 1933, 480 acres were given to the state by Dr. Travis D. Scales for use as a public recreational facility. The once strip-mined land was given a complete overhaul with major renovation by the WPA, which constructed a dam to create a lake over 60 acres in size. While originally managed as a state forest and fish hatchery, a desire by the public to use the land for outdoor recreational activities led to the property being dedicated as a state park in 1951 and officially titled Scales Lake State Beach. By the 1960s the state began decreasing its attention on state beaches, and the much larger Harmonie State Park close by further diminished the state's interest in managing the property. In 1969, Scales Lake State Beach was turned over to Warrick County to be managed as a county park.

In 1952, Indiana dedicated Kankakee State Park as its eighteenth state park property. Consisting of 1,800 acres, the tract served as a park for 12 years, featuring hiking in its southern section and rental cabins and park facilities in its northern section. Located in a marshland along the Kankakee River, the property was once publicized as a source for some of the best fishing and birdwatching in the area. As a remnant of the once great Kankakee swamp, the park's marshy characteristics prevented the park from ever being very popular. While the property gained an additional 1,200 acres, by 1963 visitation lingered around 11,678 for the year, and the property was thought to be better suited as a fish and game area. The following year the property was transferred to the Division of Fish and Game and today is managed as the Kankakee Fish and Wildlife Area—preserving 4,095 acres of open water, marsh, and riparian timber, as well as 11 miles of river.

In 1947, the Army Corp of Engineers began acquiring land as part of the Flood Control Act of 1938. By 1948, a reservoir was constructed, creating Cagles Mill Lake by 1953. First known as Cagles Mill State Forest, Indiana's Division of Forestry transferred the property to the Division of State Parks three years later, changing the name to Cataract Lake State Recreation Area. Two years later, 561 acres on the northeast section of the property was established as Richard Lieber State Park. As land acquisition continued, the combination of Cagles Mill Flood Control Reservoir, Richard Lieber State Park, and the lake leased from the Army Corp of Engineers led to the Division of Reservoir Management administering an area of over 8,000 acres. Today, the fragmented properties of various names are managed as state recreational areas and no longer carry the title of state park.

Reservoirs such as Cataract Lake, leased to the state from the Army Corp of Engineers, created a complicated situation of how the properties should be managed. Since they could not be managed under state park guidelines, the Division of Reservoir Management was created within Indiana's Department of Natural Resources to help maintain recreational activities on large reservoirs. In 1961, Indiana's twenty-first state park

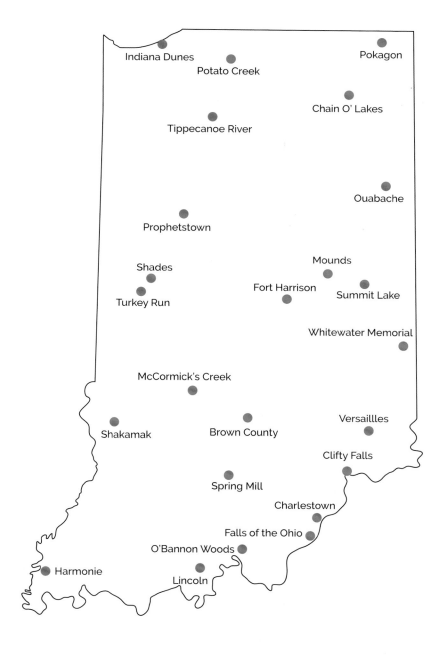

Indiana Dunes
Potato Creek
Pokagon
Chain O' Lakes
Tippecanoe River
Ouabache
Prophetstown
Mounds
Shades
Fort Harrison
Summit Lake
Turkey Run
Whitewater Memorial
McCormick's Creek
Versaillles
Shakamak
Brown County
Clifty Falls
Spring Mill
Charlestown
Falls of the Ohio
O'Bannon Woods
Harmonie
Lincoln

was dedicated on a similar reservoir as Cataract Lake known as Raccoon Lake. As with Richard Lieber State Park, Raccoon Lake eventually lost its title as a state park and was changed to be managed as Raccoon Lake State Recreation Area under the newly created Division of Reservoir Management. In 1996, the Division of Reservoir Management merged with the Division of State Parks. Seven of the reservoirs built by the Corps of Engineers and one state lake are now part of the Division of State Parks.

INDIANA STATE NATURE PRESERVES

Indiana currently has over 250 nature preserves, many of which are on state park property or adjoined in close proximity to a park. While not all of Indiana's nature preserves are owned by the Department of Natural Resources, those connected to the state park system help rare or endangered species return to state park property. The foundation for creating Indiana's nature preserves began with the creation of the 1967 Nature Preserves Act, which aided in giving further protection for rare species of plants and animals and any other areas deemed to have "unusual natural significance." Set aside as natural museums, nature preserves' most important feature is to retain the land to presettlement conditions. Having strict guidelines on how human interaction occurs in these areas, some nature preserves are even closed to the public. How a nature preserve operates to the public is often policed by the property's owners, which in most cases would be The Nature Conservancy. Instrumental in conserving state lands, The Nature Conservancy currently protects Indiana's more than 60 state nature preserves, some of which are managed by Indiana's state parks. ACRES Land Trust has also shared a great deal of the responsibility and stories of success to save and protect vital parts of Indiana. With close to a dozen other land trusts and private partners involved with raising the necessary funds and acquiring land for protection, thousands of acres have been set aside for future generations. While establishing a nature preserve can be a daunting task, once a preserve is dedicated the land within its borders is protected forever from any form of development. Indiana's Division of Nature Preserves serves as the lead in ensuring that the protected tracts of land continue to remain in pristine condition by administering prescribed burns, removing invasive species, and maintaining the properties' borders and trails. Two programs within the Division of Nature Preserves, the Indiana Natural

Heritage Data Center and the Lake Michigan Coastal Program, help keep track of the rare species that exist within preserve property while enhancing how the state manages its natural and cultural resources. The first nature preserve to be dedicated in the state was Pine Hills Nature Preserve in 1969, located in Shades State Park. Today, the Division of Nature Preserves celebrates close to 50 years in operation while protecting over 50,000 acres of land throughout Indiana.

HORSES AND SADDLE BARNS AT INDIANA STATE PARKS

While long used as work animals and to carry people, equipment, and supplies prior to the overwhelming popularity of motorized vehicles, horses and saddle barns have been a staple of Indiana since settlers first arrived to the area. Indiana State Park saddle barns offer visitors the opportunity to see the natural beauty of its properties from a different perspective by providing trail rides and horse-riding lessons. While located on state park property, saddle barns are operated by independent contractors who often lease the facilities. The trails at many state parks are often unique, some offering horse-only trails, while others offer multiuse trails with horses sharing the path with hikers. Some state parks offer camping options for horse owners and allow those visitors to freely roam independently throughout the park. However, if renting a horse for a unique trail riding experience is more what you are looking for, the following state parks offer saddle barns and horse rentals (check with the parks themselves for details, as services come and go):

> Brown County State Park
> Fort Harrison State Park
> McCormick's Creek State Park
> Pokagon State Park
> Turkey Run State Park
> Whitewater Memorial State Park

STATE PARK FRIENDS GROUPS

Many of Indiana's state parks have a friends group or volunteer organization established to help maintain its park and help raise money for new facilities. With the nation's budget for recreational facilities, parks, and natural areas at an all-time low, each park depends on volunteers to ease the stress of operating thousands of acres of public land with a minimal staff. Aside from maintaining trails, these groups have successfully raised money for new educational buildings and helped save, salvage, and rebuild old structures, such as CCC fire towers. If you love and appreciate a particular state park near your home or have fond memories of visiting a particular park, get involved with one or more of the state's registered 501(c) nonprofit friends group organizations. While some state parks do not have a dedicated friends group, volunteer opportunities exist at every state park. Contact state park staff directly for more information about volunteer opportunities that exist in your area.

"Our state parks preserve the sources of our inspiration. Their purpose is not merely to satisfy but to uplift."

—RICHARD LIEBER

THE COMPLETE GUIDE TO

INDIANA
STATE PARKS

1

McCormick's Creek State Park

Established 1916—1,961 acres

250 McCormick's Creek Park Road

Spencer, IN 47460

(812) 829-2235

39.294444, -86.727778

The region was at one time settled by Miami, Delaware, Potawatomi, and Eel River Indians who are thought to have hunted and made camps along the White River and McCormick's Creek. During the era of European settlement, the land was first acquired by John McCormick on September 20, 1816. McCormick never visited the land, but his two sons Thomas and Hudson operated mills on the creek, and his daughter Nancy, with her husband Jesse Peden, raised livestock and chickens, had a vegetable garden, and farmed hundreds of acres of wheat. In order to keep milk, butter, and eggs from spoiling, a springhouse was constructed, using old-fashioned ingenuity and the local geology to keep the building cold. Using the cold water from a spring, milk cans were placed in a trough to keep cool while butter and eggs were placed on shelves around the building.

When Jesse and Nancy's son Tom took over the farm, he constructed a large barn after the farm's original log barn burned down in 1857. The new barn, of massive proportion, was set on top of gigantic limestone pillars assembled by a stonemason from England. Large hickory timbers, 64 feet long, stretched the length of the pillars. As years passed, the land became a patchwork of smaller farms and properties, leaving barns and a schoolhouse to decay. Artemus Pratt's five-room home once stood where the Beech Grove Shelter currently resides. Sidney Henrick lived in a home just above McCormick's Creek Falls on the ridge, while his brother James owned a home where the Canyon Inn now stands. Near the McCormick's Creek Falls parking area, the Laymon family owned a five-room home with a log barn just west of the house. Fredrick Denkewalter continued to add to the structure, creating a hodge podge building known as the Denkewalter Sanitarium. Near the park superintendent's house, an original settler to the area named Dunn had a home, and Harrison Bean built a two-room home near the campgrounds near Trail 7. The one-room schoolhouse was located near the old stone bridge and at one time had 96 students enrolled at the school. With so many pupils, there was not enough room for desks, so benches were built around the interior walls.

QUARRY

When the Great Chicago fire devastated that city in 1871, the demands for limestone increased. In 1878 the Statehouse Quarry, a limestone quarry built on a bluff of solid stone along McCormick's Creek, began operating on what is now park property. Stone cut from the land was used for the foundation and basement of the capitol building in Indianapolis. The limestone boom hit as railroads capable of hauling the heavy stone were built across the state, and the newly invented channeling machine was used to cut the stone vertically with ease. Workdays were 10 hours long, and the quarry once employed 50 to 75 men at one time. A village of 13 buildings was located at the quarry site providing the workers a close place to live. Married men were provided private huts for their families, and single men were given a space in dormitory housing. Once considered one of the finest of its time, the quarry operated for two years before the operation was abandoned due to the constant washing out of the train trestle over the White River. Remains from the operation are still visible, including the old railroad trestle across the White River, which was used to ship the heavy stone, as well as a bridge foundation at the creek near the quarry.

During the late 1800s many towns began promoting the naturally occurring mineral waters for their rejuvenating nature. While recovering from sunstroke, an Indianapolis physician and minister named Fredrick Denkewalter visited the countryside seeking fresh air and a peaceful setting. Taken by the area, he later returned in 1880 and purchased 90 acres of McCormick's old property. His land purchase also included an old farmhouse located not far from McCormick's Creek Falls. With the intention of building a place of solace, he converted the old farmhouse into a sanitarium designed to offer others a place to rest, relax, and recuperate within the peaceful setting of nature. Due to demand by the public, Denkewalter had to enlarge the structure twice, eventually purchasing a total of 374 acres and selling his medical practice to operate the health resort full time. During the boom of the mineral water craze, health spas and sanitariums also opened in the nearby towns of Spencer, Gosport, and Martinsville, promoting the therapeutic benefits of the area's natural settings. With the death of Denkewalter in 1914, his children decided to sell the property at a public auction. With debate from the citizens of Owen County about converting the land into a public park, Richard Lieber was approached to work with the people of Owen County and the state of Indiana to raise the funds necessary to purchase the sanitarium and the property surrounding the canyon. With the influence of Richard Lieber, McCormick's Creek State Park was purchased by the state by combining state funds with money from Owen County. Officially established on July 4, 1916, McCormick's Creek became Indiana's first state park, setting a standard of distinction that remains to present day. Colonel Richard Lieber, being an advocate of protecting natural areas for their therapeutic benefits, relished the idea of McCormick's Creek being used as a quiet place to revitalize people. Returning multiple times throughout his life, he died in one of the rooms of the Canyon Inn in 1944. Over the years the park continued to increase in size, with the last large land purchase of the Deer Run area occurring in 1951. Today the park stands at 1,961 acres.

The park's premiere lodging, Canyon Inn, once served not only as a farmhouse but also as an orphanage for a short time before being purchased by Fredrick Denkewalter. After being taken over by the state of Indiana for a park, the inn underwent many changes and renovations. First remodeled by the park in 1922, a brick wing and entryway was later added in 1932. The original wooden structure of the inn was torn down in 1941 and replaced with a matching brick addition. Today the beautiful structure has stood the test of time for over 100 years, offering visitors six different types of rooms with 76 guest rooms and two conference areas.

Canyon Inn.

CCC

The Civilian Conservation Corps (CCC) Company 589 was assigned to work and live at McCormick's Creek from November 1933 until July 1935—beginning the first construction of the park's gatehouse in 1934. The original CCC camp had eight barracks, a recreation hall, vehicle storage building, a mess hall, and several administration buildings. Other tasks included installing water lines, building many of the hiking trails, and constructing the often-overlooked Stone Arch Bridge. The bridge was said to be a masterpiece of stone masonry for its time and features the use of a center keystone that compresses the bridge's archway, holding the structure together. With a 50-foot span, the bridge's highest point stands 25 feet over the creek below. Today it remains the only self-supporting bridge built by the CCC in Indiana. When the CCC left the park in 1935, the recreation hall was converted into a nature museum and was used for over 30 years to highlight the park's native landscape. The nature museum was later used for storage before being converted to a rentable facility. One of the more notable members of the CCC camp was Euclid Dearing. While first assigned to work on the park's gatehouse and original driveway, he was later assigned to work as the camp's cook. A dedicated member of the CCC, Euclid worked in the park and later became a key component in the restoration of the park and CCC reunions in

Stone Arch Bridge originally built by the Civilian Conservation Corps.

his later years. The amphitheater was constructed by the Works Progress Administration in 1936. The famous Stone Arch Bridge, park gatehouse, and CCC recreation hall/nature museum were all added to the National Register of Historic Places in 1993.

GEOLOGY

The park and most of its key features tend to center around the diverse geology of the landscape. The limestone used to build most of the park's buildings and bridges represents just how limestone rich the area is, while the sinkholes, the cave, and falls show what water and time can do to the ancient stone.

The limestone geology and karst topography of the area create many interesting rock formations.

MCCORMICK'S CREEK FALLS

Created from the unique existence of two types of limestone, McCormick's Creek Falls was formed as water flowed over the upper, harder, less easily dissolved limestone while eroding away the lower softer layer of limestone that forms the falls and lower creek bed.

SWIMMING POOL

The park's first swimming pool was constructed in 1928 and was originally spring fed.

WOLF CAVE NATURE PRESERVE

Located in the northeast section of the park, the Wolf Cave Nature Preserve protects the Wolf Cave and the majority of Litten's Branch. Within the secluded valley, a mixture of tree types exist, including American beech along the area's cool slopes; sycamore, red elm, and black walnut in the drier valleys; and chinquapin, red and white oak, and shagbark hickory in the drier upland ridges. The areas around Litten's Branch also contain a large collection of mosses, liverworts, and ferns. Trail 5 leads through the entire expanse of the preserve, offering visitors an opportunity to explore Wolf Cave.

MCCORMICK'S COVE NATURE PRESERVE

The park's southwestern corner containing the old quarry site and family cabins is protected by McCormick's Cove Nature Preserve—a 177-acre tract, old-growth, floodplain forest. Lindsey, Schmeltz, and Nichols first recognized McCormick's Cove Nature Preserve as a significant natural area in their 1969 book, *Natural Areas in Indiana and Their Preservation*. During a 1985 inventory of Owen County, McCormick's Cove was described as "probably the best mesic and dry-mesic forest seen in the county." Due to the diverse soil conditions, the area flourishes with a wide variety of wildflowers, ferns, and woody species.

McCormick's Creek Falls.

NATURE CENTER

One of the finest nature centers in the state, a large collection of displays educate on the park's history, geology, animal life, and flora. The CCC is well represented with vintage artifacts and a video, as well as a display about park interpretation.

NATURE CENTER HABITAT TRAIL

(0.14 miles)—The path begins at the northeast corner of the nature center and has 12 labeled stations, educating the public on topics such as trees, herbs, and wildlife. A pamphlet is available from the center that goes into more detail about each station and the successional forest. The trail ends at the southwest corner of the nature center.

TRAIL 1—CABIN LOOP FOREST TRAIL

(0.5 miles) Moderate—The trail begins and ends at the family cabins looping though the western edge of the park and through McCormick's Cove Nature Preserve.

TRAIL 2—MCCORMICK'S CREEK OVERLOOK TRAIL

(1.0 miles) Moderate—The trail begins at the CCC recreation hall and leads northwest into the northern section of McCormick's Cove Nature Preserve before turning south and ending at the family cabins. Trail 1 can be picked up from there. The trail passes several access points to other trails and serves as a good starting point to other trails throughout the park.

TRAIL 3—MCCORMICK'S CREEK TRAIL

(0.8 miles) Rugged—The path can be accessed at several points, including Stoney Restroom near the amphitheater or from the parking lot near McCormick's Creek Falls. A connector trail creates a loop, ending the trail near the Recreation Center and Canyon Inn.

TRAIL 4—FIRE TOWER TRAIL

(1.4 miles) Moderate—McCormick's Creek is one of the few parks to still have a fire tower. Located on Trail 4, the 86-foot-tall structure with a seven-by-seven-foot cab was first constructed in 1935 by the CCC. Regularly used until 1967, the tower was officially listed on the National Historic Lookout Register on November 12, 2008.

TRAIL 5—WOLF CAVE TRAIL

(2.0 miles) Moderate—The trails of McCormick's Creek are scattered with large sinkholes—a result of the area's water eroding the limestone-rich landscape. Wolf Cave and Twin Bridges seen along Trail 5 are just a few of the outcomes the erosive power of water can create. While no longer housing wolves, the cave gets its name from a story about Nancy Peden being chased by wolves after passing the entrance of the cave. It is said that she survived by throwing down her bonnet and gloves to distract the wolves, allowing her to make it home safely. The cave was once closed to protect the spread of white-nose syndrome in bats. The cave was reopened in May 2014 and remains a fascinating stop for visitors, with its long winding corridor that leads to a modest-sized room. Unlike most of the caves in Indiana that have been closed, Wolf Cave's size, location, and lack of use by bats allowed the cave to continue to be used by visitors. Twin Bridges once formed a larger chamber of Wolf Cave, until the roof collapsed and the remaining parts of the chamber formed the limestone bridges we see today. The trail also passes a large portion of Wolf Cave Nature Preserve, which is protected as a nature preserve due to the importance of the area's subterranean features.

TRAIL 6—CAMPGROUND WOODLAND TRAIL

(0.6 miles) Easy—The trail loops from the east side of the campground to the Beech Grove Shelter. The short hike and easy access from the campground makes it a very popular trek for overnight visitors—leading primarily north and south near the youth tent area and the primitive camping area.

TRAIL 7—WHITE RIVER TRAIL

(1.8 miles) Moderate—The trail offers views of White River and McCormick's Creek with enormous sycamores and a long, wooden platform sprawling through the woods. Another trail that is very close to the western edge of the campground, the path follows a service road for a short distance on the northern section, while giving an easy access point to Trail 10 and the Old Quarry along the southern section.

TRAIL 8—CAMPGROUND/POOL CONNECTOR TRAIL

(0.7 miles) Easy and Accessible—A paved path, located between campsites 14 and 15, connects the campground to the swimming pool and bathhouse, while passing two access points to Trail 5 and the Pine Bluff Shelter.

TRAIL 9—WOODLAND SINKHOLE TRAIL

(1.2 miles) Easy—The trail features the remnants of the Peden Farm Site, including several old foundations and the springhouse that was used to store food. Restored in 2012, 18 inches of mud and debris were removed from the springhouse, revealing a flowing spring, a sediment pit, and a water trough. Remnants of the legendary Peden barn also still exist. While all of the wood from the barn collapsed years ago, the enormous limestone base still remains.

TRAIL 10

(0.7 miles) Rugged—This modest connector trail joins Trail 2, Trail 5, and Trail 7, while also connecting with the Quarry Loop. It crosses McCormick's Creek three times and is one of the best trails to connect other trails in any direction, leading to all of the key features of the park.

BRIDLE TRAIL

(3.5 miles)—This trail begins and ends at the park's saddle barn, crossing McCormick's Creek in the southeastern section of the park. The smooth path leads through the flattest area of the park through a young successional forest and crosses Trail 9 near the historic Peden Farm Site and Deer Run Shelter.

2

Turkey Run State Park

Established 1916—2,382 acres

8121 E. Park Road

Marshall, IN 47859

(765) 597-2635

39.885, -87.203333

Native Americans once claimed the Sugar Creek area that is now Turkey Run State Park as their home. The creek and its densely forested tributaries connect to 30 continuous miles of diverse forest—providing an assorted ecological home to many animals that cannot survive in smaller forested habitats. Additionally, the Miami Indians once walked many of the same trails that park visitors still use today.

During a meeting of the commission that helped fund the purchase of Turkey Run, Richard Lieber was quoted as saying, "Turkey Run is a paradise of rocky gorges, glens, bathing beaches, and waterfalls, a retreat for song birds, and a garden of wildflowers. It has hundreds of magnificent black walnut, oak, poplar, and other stately trees, all growing in primeval forest which the Lusk family carefully preserved from the lumberman's axe."

THE LUSK FAMILY

During the spring of 1823, a young man named Salmon Lusk and his wife, Mary "Polly" Lusk, traveled from Terre Haute to the area of Parke County, stopping on the wild and beautiful banks of Sugar Creek. The land they intended to make their home was granted to the ex-military captain as a reward for his service in the army. Seeing the location as a paradise, they became the first European occupants of the property we now call Turkey Run. With the creek water flowing strong, the site was perfect for constructing a water-powered mill. Spring floods allowed for flatboats to be used for exporting ground corn down the river, all the way down to New Orleans. Lusk first built a log cabin along the banks of the creek, but as he prospered in business and his family grew, his sons helped build a brick home high up on the banks. As he and his family enjoyed life along the creek, a small village grew up near the Lusk property before the great Sugar Creek flood of 1847 swept away the mill and many of the buildings of the town.

When Salmon Lusk died in 1869, he left the homestead and 1,000 acres to his wife and oldest son, John Lusk. After Polly Lusk died in 1880, he became a recluse with an obsession to save the land from clear cutting or development of any kind. While he avoided any offers to buy the land, John did grant people permission to roam and enjoy the property. In 1881, he even went as far as to lease a portion of it to the Decatur & Springfield Railroad for use as a summer resort. The company built an eating house and advertised the retreat as "Bloomingdale Glens." As with many railroad companies at the time, financial reasons forced Decatur & Springfield to abandon their lease, and it was quickly given to William Hooghkirk. Operating a resort under the same name, Hooghkirk managed the resort between 1884 and 1910. At that point the lease went to R. P. Luke. Under his management the property was more popular than ever.

ACQUISITION OF THE LAND

When John Lusk died in 1915, the realization that the property might be lost forever became a great concern. Having a fond appreciation for the land, Parke County native and local writer Juliet Strauss began a campaign to save the property by writing to Governor Samuel Ralston, asking for help to save the forest from the exploitation of timber companies that had long tried to buy the property. Having worked as a columnist for the Rockville newspaper and the *Indianapolis News*, Strauss became of voice of conservation for the area, gaining the attention of Richard Lieber and Governor Ralston through her writing. Inspired by her passion, Ralston appointed Strauss to the newly formed Turkey Run Commission, along with Mr. William Watson Woollen and Miss Vide Newsom, on April 28, 1915. The following January, Richard Lieber and

Mr. Albert Cannon were added to the commission, and an investigation by the group found that the Lusk property had been divided into nine tracts—Tract No. 3 contained about 288 acres and most of the more scenic features. With no state funds to purchase the property, the commission worked tirelessly for two months before becoming inactive.

By early March, Dr. Frank B. Wynn, acting chairman of the Indiana Historical Commission, worked out a deal with Richard Lieber to form his own separate commission as well as to advance the project $1,500 to be used for a public financial campaign. Mr. Lannes McPhetridge, Sol S. Kiser, L. M. Rappaport, Wynn, and Strauss were all chosen to work on the commission, with Lieber serving as chairman. From March 18, 1916, until the land was scheduled to go to auction on May 18, 1916, the group met daily, working with the Indianapolis Board of Trade, the Indianapolis Chamber of Commerce, and local newspapers to raise $20,000 dollars to be used toward the purchase of Tract No. 3. Since the 288 acres was appraised at only $18,000, the commission anticipated a successful win of the sale, although competition was high from timber companies. On the day of the auction, 2,000 people attended and, through breathless anticipation, the cost of the property swiftly grew to $30,200, with Joseph Gross and the Hoosier Veneer Company winning the sale.

Originally proposed as Indiana's first state park, the complications with land acquisition held the project off until after McCormick's Creek was established. As a mark of his keen business skills and determination for the project, Lieber continued to help raise private funds to buy the old-growth forest and eventually worked out a deal with the Hoosier Veneer Company. Having purchased the property solely as an investment, Joseph Gross gave Richard Lieber two options: either they would sell the land untouched to the state at a profit to themselves, or the Hoosier Veneer Company would cut the most desirable trees from the property and sell the land for the same price they paid. After a substantial amount of additional fundraising, six months later the Hoosier Veneer Company arranged to sell the land to the state for $40,200, gaining a $10,000 profit.

JULIET STRAUSS MEMORIAL

No single person felt the pain of losing the property to the Hoosier Veneer Company like Juliet Strauss. Having spent her childhood roaming the hills and walking the rock-covered shores of Sugar Creek, she more than anyone held the area like a religion, holding the woods in the same regard as great temples. "I am sick of soul," she once said. "Who would have dreamed that a few men's dollars could step in and destroy all this, the most beautiful spot in Indiana, one that all the money in the world could not restore once it is gone?" When given the chance to fight for the property once again with Richard Lieber, she got in line with the rest of the community to save Turkey Run from destruction. Strauss, who died just two years after the establishment of Turkey Run State Park in 1918, was honored by the Women's Press Club of Indiana with a statue at Turkey Run State Park. This statue stands as a reminder of her contribution to Turkey Run State Park and the conservation of its forest.

COL. RICHARD LIEBER MEMORIAL

After passing in 1944, Richard Lieber's ashes were buried at a memorial to him at Turkey Run State Park with the ashes of his wife Emma and their son. A bust of Lieber is set in a lovely hemlock grove.

HISTORIC STRUCTURES—LUSK HOMESITE AND LUSK EARTH FILL

While the property began with only 288 acres, Turkey Run State Park currently preserves 2,382 acres and holds within its borders a great deal of history and historic structures. The Lusk Homesite was built by the first settlers to the area. After acquiring the land, Captain Lusk began building a gristmill that he completed in 1826. The Lusk home, completed in 1841, housed the first stewards of the land, as the Lusk family preserved the pristine landscape to similar conditions as today. The Lusk's Earth Fill was John Lusk's attempt to build a roadbed to get a county road there, while also building a fishing pond. The failed construction took three years and thousands of dollars, only to end with a disappointing dirt mound of little significance aside from a valiant tale.

LIEBER CABIN

Situated near Sunset Point is a pioneer cabin that came to the park by way of the negotiating talent of Col. Richard Lieber. While leaving Turkey Run State Park one day, Lieber made a wrong turn and found himself on a nearby property owner's land that had two unique cabins. Lieber approached the landowner about buying the better of the two cabins but was denied, since the property owner needed to use the cabin as a shed. By happenstance, Indiana State Farm prisoners were doing work in the park as a way of giving back to the community, and Lieber quickly put

On the memorial:

"ALL THINGS BY
IMMORTAL POWER,
NEAR AND FAR,

HIDDENLY TO
EACH OTHER
CONNECTED ARE;

THAT YOU
CAN'T DISTURB
A FLOWER

WITHOUT THE
TROUBLING
OF A STAR."

BORN SEPT. 5, 1869
AT ST. JOHANN
SAARBRUECKED, GERMANY
DIED APR. 15, 1944
AT MCCORMICKS CREEK STATE PARK
INDIANA

A bronze bust nestled in a curved stone wall on a quiet hillside is a memorial to Col. Richard Lieber.

the prisoners to work to build the property owner a new shed at a cost of $85. The property owner, in turn, traded the cabin to Lieber for the deed, and the state park received the cabin outright. One year later, Lieber returned to the property owner once again to attempt to get the second cabin, but he was disappointed to find that the cabin had been dismantled and burned to cook sugar. The cabin that now sits in Turkey Run is one of the oldest cabins of its kind, built around 1848 by Daniel Gay with tools consisting of only an axe and other primitive woodworking tools. During reconstruction on park property, great care was taken to retain

Built in 1919, Turkey Run Inn provides the comfort of a modern facility with the atmosphere of a rustic country inn.

the structure's original appearance. The cabin's logs are 30 feet in length, 32 inches wide, and 8 inches thick, entirely made of yellow poplar. All the doors, window casings, and the mantel are made of black walnut, while the floors are made of poplar. Oak logs make up most of the supporting structure. One of the most interesting features of the old cabin is its cat-and-clay chimney made out of sticks of white walnut and Mansfield sandstone pulled and dragged from the lower ravines of Turkey Run.

THE LOG CHURCH
Colonel Lieber moved the church, which was built in 1871 and originally located off the property at the nearby town of Oak Ridge, to Turkey Run in 1923. The church is still used as a house of worship today, and nondenominational services are conducted during the warmer months of the year every Sunday at 10:00 AM.

TURKEY RUN INN

The construction of inns at parks coincided with the dawn of the automobile, since vehicles at the time were still somewhat unreliable. A 50-mile road trip, for example, almost always entailed finding overnight accommodations, and it wasn't uncommon for people traveling the countryside to sleep in barn lofts, on porches, or in spare bedrooms of area farms. Turkey Run Inn was built in 1919, becoming the first inn constructed in Indiana's state park system. The following year, the inn was enlarged with a new wing and cabins, and by 1930 a second 32-room brick annex was added. In 1975 a swimming pool was completed, which was fully enclosed as an indoor, heated swimming pool in 1991. Today, the inn comprises 61 rooms in the main lodge, Narrows Restaurant, and rental space for meetings, and it oversees five buildings with cabin rooms, as well as three additional cabins.

NARROWS COVERED BRIDGE

The bridge at "The Narrows," as it was once referred to, was built in 1882. A single-span bridge crossing over Sugar Creek, the structure is a Burr Arch Truss design built by Joseph A. Britton and said to be the first bridge designed and built as part of Britton's illustrious bridge-building career. The bridge was built to replace two bridges built and maintained by the original landowner, Salmon Lusk; the first was destroyed in 1847 and the second in 1875. Britton's first wife died during the construction of the Narrows Bridge, and he later met his second wife before construction was complete. The bridge was added to the National Register of Historic Places in 1972.

CCC

The Civilian Conservation Corps (CCC) Company 2580, supported with a mess hall, barracks, and commissary hall, made its mark on the park in the 1930s. The CCC was tasked with building basic infrastructure, including roads and trails, as well as constructing the shelter houses, the main gatehouse, the park office, saddle barn, and the terrace at Sunset Point. The camp's commissary served as the camp's store, selling supplies and clothing to the camp employees. When the CCC left Turkey Run State Park, the commissary was converted into a concession stand offering grilled hamburgers and other food to park visitors, as well as serving as a spot for annual square dances. The commissary was finally converted into the park's nature center in 1986, with the chimneys, fireplaces, and stone walls being the only original features left from the original CCC building.

NATURE CENTER

Turkey Run State Park offers interpretive naturalist services all year long from the park's nature center, as well as a modest but informative display detailing the park's long history. Scheduled programs include hikes, planetarium programs, history talks, and evening programs. Large groups wishing to have a program just for their group should call in advance. Inquire at the park's nature center, inn, or office.

ROCKY HOLLOW/FALLS CANYON NATURE PRESERVE

For centuries the water flowing from the tributaries down into Sugar Creek have carved tortuous cavernous pathways through hundreds of feet of sandstone. The result has been an unusual and fascinating collection of rocky canyons and hollows explored by many since well before the park existed. The area just across Sugar Creek leading into the Rocky Hollow/Falls Canyon Nature Preserve has for decades been one of the more popular spots to explore due to its vast collection of trails and mysterious rock formations. Since the inception of the park, the area has only been accessed by way of a suspension bridge connecting the central part of the park on the south side of Sugar Creek to the more rugged northern expanse. For 30 years prior to the park's establishment, a makeshift ferry carried thousands of passengers over the creek to explore the rocky terrain. The first suspension bridge (of debatable length) was built by local adventurers by tossing the makeshift bridge across and fastening it to the hillsides in some unknown way. When the bridge was deemed unsafe, the Lafayette Engineering Company was contracted in 1918 to construct the park's first permanent and secure suspension bridge. A beautifully designed bridge for the time period, the four-foot-wide structure was mounted on steel cables that anchored into the natural rock on the north side of the creek, while 50-ton concrete bases supported the cables just off of the south shore. Wallace Marshall of Lafayette was given much credit for building the bridge at cost.

The first feature that visitors come to after crossing the suspension bridge is Rocky Hollow—solid walls of sandstone a hundred feet high made from centuries of rushing water. Nearby, Wedge Rock is a huge prism-shaped stone remnant that is believed to have fallen from the top of the high cliffs. Features, such as Wedge Rock, were created by frost

Distinct rock formations and canyons are the remnants of glacial meltwaters carving the sandstone bedrock at Turkey Run State Park.

wedging, a continual process of freezing and thawing of water deep inside the cracks of the sandstone along the high cliffs. These forced cracks in the stone cause the rock to widen and fracture, causing features like Wedge Rock to separate and forming similar features in the park, such as Ice Box and Box Canyon.

The rock features and the thousands of ferns that abound in the area serve as an entry point into the long, stretching, looping trails that wind through the venturesome Rocky Hollow/Falls Canyon Nature Preserve.

A collection of well-placed ladders transition the trail out of Bear Hollow at Turkey Run State Park.

Exploring the western section of the preserve leads hikers into some of the more interesting and more secluded features, such as Ice Box, Falls Canyon, and Boulder Canyon, while circling around Bear Hollow. Other notable features abound throughout the canyons, such as Camel's Back, Box Canyon, and Newby Gulch.

ICE BOX

Like so many other places, the Devil's Ice Box, as it was known back in the day, has a history attached to it. The feature has a very appropriate name, since it is impossible for the sun to ever cast its rays deep within the hole, leaving the environment constantly cool like a refrigerator.

BEAR HOLLOW
The western section of the Rocky Hollow/Falls Canyon Nature Preserve was the toughest location to get to when the park was first established and only saw a few thousand Turkey Run visitors before antiquated trails could be replaced. Similar to Rocky Hollow, Bear Hollow is difficult to explore.

FALLS CANYON AND BOULDER CANYON
Located in the western section of the Rocky Hollow/Falls Canyon Nature Preserve, the two canyons are impressive and beautiful sites, containing the best examples of water-worn rounded boulders and prehistoric glacial activity.

GYPSY GULCH
During the days when the Lusk family owned the property, the area of Gypsy Gulch, known to the pioneers as "The Falls," was used for picnics and exploring. Visiting the area one can see why the Lusk family chose to picnic there, since it remains one of the most attractive places in the park. According to the park, Gypsy Gulch was named after Juliet Strauss whose father called her his "Gypsy Girl" due to her playing and spending time as a child in Turkey Run.

GOOSE ROCK
Located on Trail 1, along the southern shore of Sugar Creek, is a fascinating feature called Goose Rock. The name of the rock refers to its shape, which is said to resemble the head of a goose when viewed from the east on Trail 1.

COAL MINE
Vast deposits of coal still exist in the area and are still visible in the rock faces throughout the park. The coal mine located along the edge of Sugar Creek was used by the Lusk family for many years as a means of heating their home. Now permanently closed, a gate was placed on the entrance of the shaft in 2000 to protect Indiana's bat population.

CABINS AND CAMPGROUNDS
Cabins are available for rent as are 176 camping sites with electric and 2 youth tent sites. Other facilities include a nature center with several informative exhibits and an inn with a restaurant.

The hiking experiences at Turkey Run State Park are beyond the realm of many other state parks. With a diverse collection of plants, nestled among a forest hundreds of years old, there is no other place in the state that compares. The park offers 11 hiking trails, totaling 14.7 miles, which traverse a landscape of shaded forest, canyons, and intertwining stream beds. Once a prehistoric swamp, the amazing scenery is attributed to glacial meltwaters cutting through the land, exposing the Mansfield sandstone canyons. Since wind and water erosion has slowed, the gorges are very similar to what was seen by the area's first settlers and Native Americans.

Water tranquilly flows through the canyons of Turkey Run State Park.

TRAIL 1

(3 miles) Moderate/Rugged—This long trail connects the suspension bridge over Sugar Creek in the central part of the park to the easternmost edge of the park. The trail runs parallel to Sugar Creek, with a connector trail leading to the Newby Gulch Shelter, while passing several connections with Trail 2 and Goose Rock.

TRAIL 2

(2 miles) Rugged—The trail is accessed by either hiking east on Trail 1 near the Newby Gulch Shelter and the Canyon Shelter and Picnic Area, or from the Narrows Covered Bridge in the easternmost section of the park. The loop trail passes some of the park's key features, such as Box Canyon, Gypsy Gulch, and Lusk Earth Fill.

TRAIL 3

(1.7 miles) Very Rugged—The path is a connector trail passing through the park's most popular hiking area, featuring Rocky Hollow Canyon and Wedge Rock, and connects Trail 4 to two sections of Trail 10 before leading to Sugar Creek. Once at Sugar Creek, the trail runs parallel with the creek and gives access to Ice Box.

TRAIL 4

(2 miles) Moderate/Rugged—This long, looping trail leads through the northeastern section of the park and the Rocky Hollow/Falls Canyon Nature Preserve. Main features of the trail include the Lusk Homesite in the eastern section, and the old quarry and coal mine along Sugar Creek in the southern section of the trail.

TRAIL 5

(0.7 miles) Moderate—This short looping trail heads around Bear Hollow, passing the opening to Falls Canyon in the west and down "140 steps" along its eastern section.

TRAIL 6

(0.5 miles) Moderate/Rugged—The path is a popular hike through a steep canyon near Turkey Run Inn, leading past the Lieber Cabin and Turkey Run Hollow. Sunset Point resides on the northern section of the trail, overlooking Sugar Creek.

TRAIL 7

(0.7 miles) Moderate—This loop trail is accessed from the western section of Trail 6 leads through virgin woods and hemlock trees, connecting with the campground.

TRAIL 8

(1.5 miles) Moderate—This looping trail, centrally located with Trail 4, connects the old coal mine near Sugar Creek to the eastern section of Trail 4.

TRAIL 9

(1 mile) Very Rugged—Accessed from the western section of Trail 5, it comprises the most western section of the Rocky Hollow/Falls Canyon Nature Preserve, leading through Falls Canyon and Boulder Canyon before returning to Trail 5.

TRAIL 10

(1.4 miles) Moderate—Accessed from Trail 3, the trail loops north through the Rocky Hollow/Falls Canyon Nature Preserve while passing a spur trail to Camel's Back along the way.

TRAIL 11

(0.5 miles) Easy—The path is a short hike from the Turkey Run Inn parking area and leads over the old highway bridge to the Log Church and the Colonel Lieber memorial.

3

Clifty Falls State Park

Established 1920—1,519 acres

2221 Clifty Drive

Madison, IN 47250

(812) 273-8885

38.74816, -85.41523

Indiana's Internal Improvements Act in 1836 spurred economic growth for the state—as many people traveled west through the Ohio River Valley heading along newly constructed roads, canals, and railways toward the capital city of Indianapolis and beyond. Between 1836 and 1847, Indiana began focusing a great deal of money toward connecting major westward expansion routes by creating the Madison and Indianapolis Railroad Company, in hopes of building on what was the "cutting edge" of transportation technology of the time. Building a railway west of Madison was a formidable challenge due to the dangerously steep terrain and a 400-foot elevation change west of Madison and out of the Ohio River Valley.

In 1852, an Ohio entrepreneur named John Brough purchased the Madison and Indianapolis Railroad under the agreement that he would organize the construction of a railroad route to alleviate the weakest link of the proposed project—designing the railroad to run from Madison, westward up Clifty Canyon, and then east to Dean's Branch to connect to a main rail line. With over 700 men on hand, a 7,000-foot incline was cleared; two tunnels were quarried from the earth through tough, wild canyon cliffs; and stone trestles were constructed with the help of

Rue anemone grow from the cracks of the rock-lined canyon walls.

animals prior to the invention of dynamite and power equipment. After only two years and $300,000 invested, construction ceased in 1854 when the 7,000-foot incline proved to be too steep for the locomotives of the day, and Brough's Madison and Indianapolis Railroad Company declared bankruptcy. With no steel track in place and no sign of a railroad ever going through the area, the failed project became known as "Brough's Folly," after John Brough's failure to finish.

After Indiana's first two state parks officially opened, the popularity of recreational land drastically increased. In October of 1917, famed photographer Frank M. Hohenberger captured some of the first professional images of the falls and beautiful landscapes of the area—coinciding with a group of local businessmen from Madison, Indiana, exploring the possibility of a state park within the boundaries of their county. While three locations were inspected as possible sites, the natural aesthetic design, four natural waterfalls, and abandoned railroad remnants of Clifty Falls made it an ideal location for a park. Private groups, business people, organizations, and citizens of Madison collected $15,000 for the purchase of the land, and in August of 1920, Governor Goodwich approved a matching amount of state funds to acquire the first 400-acre tract, with more

Water flowing down the steep hills of Clifty Canyon provide a valuable water source for the plants and animals below.

land to be added later. With the help of Richard Lieber, Indiana's third park was established, and by the following year the park was appraised, fully appropriated, and construction began on the site's rocky terrain. Rather than tear out the existing infrastructure left from the railroad company, the area's roads, buildings, and recreational sites were left to conform to the topography over time. This allowed the park to preserve what natural beauty remained and keep a snapshot of the land's history in historical landmarks. For years the park consisted of 617 acres, but in 1965 the park acquired the nearby upland fields from the Madison State Hospital. This addition along with other gains in recent years brings the park total to 1,519 acres.

Resting high atop a bluff sits the historic Clifty Inn and Restaurant. Since first opening its doors in August 1924, the inn has dramatically changed in appearance and size, growing from a few dozen rooms to 63 rooms and 7 spectacular suites. Despite the economic downturn of the Great Depression and gas rationing during World War II, Clifty Inn has continued to be a popular destination due to its close proximity to Indianapolis, Cincinnati, and Louisville. The inn's restaurant has historically offered guests amazing food, with former inn manager Joe McDonald setting a standard during World War II, offering guests a full-course meal of chicken, mashed potatoes, vegetables, salad, freshly baked rolls, and fabulous desserts. Even while meat was scarce during the war, McDonald was known to drive the countryside searching for chickens to serve his guests for the next day's meal. In 1964, a more modern motel and pool replaced the original inn, but in 1974 a devastating tornado ripped through the park, and the motel had to be replaced. As part of a multimillion-dollar park upgrade in 2006, the present inn contains a full-scale restaurant and conference center, offering guests panoramic views of the Ohio River and the city of Madison. Famous celebrities known to have stayed at the inn include First Lady Eleanor Roosevelt in 1934, while she was in Madison to see the local Civilian Conservation Corps (CCC) in action during the Depression.

Between 1933 and 1940, the CCC had two camps staged at Clifty Falls State Park. Major projects conducted by Company 540 include the construction of the north and south gatehouses, which continue to be the main entrance points by visitors today, as well as the Clifty Shelter, South Hill Entrance Road, and the Lilly Memorial Lookout. Constructed out of large pieces of native stone for James Watkinson Lilly, who passed away on June 22, 1925, the memorable south-facing overlook and stone facade were placed by the CCC and the state of Indiana in 1927 to honor the public-spirited individual who helped create the heritage of the park. The park's saddle barn, also built by the CCC, is an important focal point that continues to be enjoyed by new generations. Built in 1938, the saddle barn was constructed of native timber and stone and once was home to a dozen or so horses cared for by park staff and used to carry visitors throughout the park. During the 1950s, the barn housed the park's famous stallion named "Champ." Operation as a barn ended in 1974 because of tornado damage. While the barn itself only suffered minor damage, nearby facilities and the horse trail system in the Ohio River Valley were devastated. The following year work began to convert the barn into an interpretive nature center. After construction, the center was officially dedicated as a nature center in 1981. Today, the center is the home office to the park's interpretive staff, with walls that are covered with displays showcasing the history of the park. Several live animal displays exist, as well as a separate room that offers birdwatching through a large window.

CLIFTY CANYON NATURE PRESERVE

The park features four waterfalls—Tunnel Falls (83 feet), Hoffman Falls (78 feet), Little Clifty Falls (60 feet), and Big Clifty Falls (60 feet)—all of which reside within the Clifty Canyon Nature Preserve. The preserve, which is located along the northwestern edge of the park, is 179 acres and offers ecological and geological highlights, such as steep cliff lines and fossils throughout its trails and creek beds. To protect both visitors and the environment, hiking and climbing is prohibited off trail and above or below the waterfalls, and the collection of wood is illegal in order to maintain the forest's natural humus development. The area is primarily made up of a mesic forest in the lower bottomlands, with dry oak-hickory forests on the upper slopes. Steep ravines support cliff communities of mosses, lichens, and ferns, with wildflowers and rare plants widespread throughout the preserve.

The waterfalls and wet pathways of Clifty Creek are formed on an erosion-resistant layer of dolomitic limestone, sandwiched between softer, more easily eroded shales—wearing away from the Ohio at a rate of one-quarter inch per year. While Big Clifty Falls presently stands at 60 feet and is located two and a half miles upstream from the Ohio River, it is believed that 250,000 years ago the falls was located only a few hundred feet from the Ohio River.

The park offers 10 hiking trails that vary from easy to very rugged, with some of the toughest hiking in Indiana. Portions of the park's hiking trails follow the original grade of the proposed railroad, and several stone piers and trestle supports can still be seen along the hiking trails. While one of the tunnels was permanently closed at both ends due to safety reasons, the remnants of a 600-foot tunnel along Trail 5 still remain open from May until the end of October, closing in the winter months to prevent disturbance of hibernating bats.

Clifty Falls State Park is rightly named as it contains four different waterfall formations, all unique in their own beautiful way.

Shooting stars thrive along the warm and sandy cliff lines.

TRAIL 1

(0.75 miles) Rugged—Located in the most southern section of the park, the trail begins near the parking area at the nature center and heads farther south toward the Ohio River. The trail descends down a gravel pathway past old foundations, leading directly to an observation tower that was once used as a fire tower. The tower overlooks the Clifty Creek Electric Plant and the Ohio River. Descending farther down a rocky path, the trail turns north following steep grades in and out of the canyon, passing a trail intersection with Trails 2 and 3 before eventually leading north to the park road.

TRAIL 2

(3 miles) Very Rugged—The trail can be accessed at many points by many trails throughout the park and serves as a central hiking trail, leading through the area's lowest elevation and directly through the shallow waters of Clifty Creek. The canyon creek is scattered with a plethora of fossils, large stones, odd man-made creek crossings, and water-loving plants and animals. Narrow, woodland trails periodically appear along the edge of the creek, allowing the path to exit the creek's waters and follow an easy-to-hike soft-surface path through lush forest understories compacted with dozens of wildflowers. Tall, lobbing trilliums are especially predominant along the forested paths. This hike is generally rugged and tough, as one is required to constantly balance over various sizes of creek rock through flowing water. It should be noted that the trail may be impassable during times of high water and the areas above and below the waterfalls are always off limits.

TRAIL 3

(1 mile) Rugged—Serving more as a connector trail to other trails in order to form a loop, the path follows along the west-facing edge of the canyon slope along a narrow and rocky trail. Several small bridges have been built over constant water seeps flowing from the hillside. The trail works well as a way to reach Hoffman Falls from the south or the nature center from the north if hiking along Trail 2 or Trail 4.

TRAIL 4

(0.75 miles) Rugged—This path traverses a steep, rocky, and narrow ridge past breathtaking rock faces and limestone outcroppings. Native stone is a key component of this particular trail, as several collections of stone steps have been built into the hillside in order to aid in descending the steep terrain. Scattered along the edges of the trail, stone foundations still hold their shape as evidence of Brough's Trace and the Madison and Indianapolis Railroad trestle that was built using only the power of man and animal. The stone steps that the path continues to lead over are also a reminder of human endurance, as they were all carved and placed by hand.

TRAIL 5

(0.9 miles) Rugged—Several parking areas have been designed with westward trails that lead directly downhill due to their importance to the tale of Brough's Folly and the failed railroad construction that created a 600-foot tunnel, which the trail passes. The hillside is scattered with stone steps and colorful dolomite rock traveling along a west-facing, rocky path. Enormous, sheer rock faces line the upper hillsides, and the area is scattered with large boulders that are remnants of the hill's eroding facade. Below the Oak Grove Shelter, the tunnel is open on both ends but is closed November 1 through April 31 in order to protect hibernating bats. Each opening of the tunnel is surrounded by large, eroded stone, making the trek into the tunnel particularly difficult. A spur trail on the northern end near the tunnel leads down to Clifty Creek and Trail 2.

TRAIL 6

(0.5 miles) Moderate/Rugged—The trail can be accessed at the Hickory Grove parking area and leads northwest along the steep canyon edge, just below the rim of Lookout Point. Running parallel with the park road, the trail eventually connects with Trail 7.

TRAIL 7

(1.25 miles) Moderate/Rugged—Regarded as one of the best short-loop trails, the path is very well maintained and heavily lined with wood and stone steps for ease of hiking to two of the park's most notable waterfalls—Big Clifty and Little Clifty Falls. Located near the north gate of the park and a very nice recreational area, the trail is accessed by two main points close to the Clifty Shelter. The west side of the parking area begins the path with an additional spur trail leading below the cliff line for an additional view of Clifty Falls. While this spur trail once led the path under a dangerous outcropping, the trail has since been designed as a dead end, with its existing stone railing and a brick wall. The main path of Trail 7 meanders south, passing a large, pivoted stone formation known as Cake Rock. Due to the wet conditions of the area, the trail is lush with ferns, mosses, and wildflowers—including columbine, which thrives on rocky surfaces. Immediately after Cake Rock, the trail leads north, crossing over Little Clifty Falls. On the other side of the falls, a flat, heavily trampled area gives visitors a distant view of the falls. Here the trail leads south to Trail 6 or north to continue Trail 7 along a meandering, woodland path over wooden bridges with the sound of rushing water. The trail exits at the paved, park road, looping around the recreational area just east of the Clifty Shelter.

TRAIL 8

(4.5 miles) Rugged—The path begins just west of the north gatehouse and leads south along the west rim of Clifty Canyon. Steep grades at the north and south ends of the trail lead the path up to a smooth ridgeline hiking experience. A steep switchback adjacent to the Oak Grove parking area leads down to Clifty Creek and Trail 2. The trail traverses the most western edge of the Clifty Canyon Nature Preserve and includes nice views of the west-facing forests of the park, as well as long overlooks of the Clifty Creek below. Once on top of the ridge, the trail is mostly an easy hike along a wide woodland path, filled with a thick forest understory of dozens of wildflower species, as well as native shrubs and tall, shady trees. The south end of the trail crosses over several wooden bridges that span flowing tributaries before the trail leads downhill, connecting with the most southern point of Trail 2.

TRAIL 9

(1 mile) Moderate—This moderately flat and grassy path connects the campground to the swimming pool and Clifty Inn, and onward south to the nature center. The path crosses portions of Hoffman's Branch, a tributary to Clifty Creek, and has water seasonally. More of a recreational connector trail to park facilities, the path is a perfect route connecting most of the park's best family features.

TRAIL 10

(0.75 miles) Easy—Beginning behind the swimming pool parking area, the trail includes a utility connector path about halfway, initially creating two adjoined loop paths. A spur trail leads west to the Trail 3 parking area and is very close to the recreational facilities of Poplar Grove Shelter and Hoffman Falls. Known as a short, family loop, Trail 10 offers many opportunities to explore old field ecology.

4

Indiana Dunes State Park

Established 1925—2,182 acres

1600 N. 25 E.

Chesterton, IN 46304

(219) 926-1952

41.66, -87.04

Located at the most northwestern part of the state, Indiana Dunes is a unique and diverse place, created over the course of 12,000 years from southern-directed wind and water currents. The lake waters that make the area so magical came to be by the melting of the last of three glaciers to pass through the area during the Pleistocene Ice Age. What has transpired in that time is a landscape that not only contains sandy beach but also towering sand mounds, directly connected to rich forest woodlands and low-lying tamarack bogs. Always in a constant state of change dating back to the glacial movement, the dunes are the result of the rising and lowering of Lake Michigan, creating a broad and gentle shoreline known as the Toleston Beach Ridge.

Historically the area was first used as a hunting ground by the Potawatomi and Miami Native American tribes, who visited primarily in the summer months. Choosing to live in the woods south of the area, those ancient tribes might find it odd that today the shoreline is scattered with summer homes and campgrounds. While the Miami tribes first moved into the area continuing south of the dunes in the late 1670s, the Potawatomi moved in from lower Michigan around 1681—making

Remnants of fallen trees scatter the upper sandy ridges along the dunes shoreline.

the area their home for the next 150 years, until they were shipped off to Mississippi by the US government.

Nestled next to the second largest Great Lake, the area surrounding Indiana Dunes State Park played an important role in maritime trade and commerce, which it continues to this day. The botanical significance of the dunes cannot be stressed enough since 26 percent of the plants that are endangered or threatened in Indiana exist within the borders of the Indiana Dunes National Lakeshore—with many thriving just on the edges of their natural range. Biological interest in the area dates back to the 1800s when Henry Chandler Cowles of the University of

The Indiana Dunes State Park inland forests provide a habitat for ferns and other shade-loving plants.

Chicago used the area as a laboratory to study the plants of Indiana Dunes. Studying pioneer plant transition to upland forests, his research developed into what is now the understanding of plant succession and modern ecology. Further educational involvement from the public continued well into the 1900s as the Prairie Club of Chicago began leading guided hikes through the dunes, an activity that grew in popularity such that a special train was designed to transport members.

As industrialization began to move in, groups such as the Prairie Club, as well as local activists and artists, saw the need to preserve the land before it could be destroyed. The preservation of the dunes and the establishment of a park first sprouted from the actions of passionate individuals. Letters from these involved citizens eventually caught the attention of influential state politicians, and after visiting the area,

Richard Lieber was on board as well. With his influence and the hard work already done by the local activists, Lieber was able to secure 2,182 acres along three miles of shoreline in order to conserve the area for Indiana Dunes State Park. While Lieber was able to secure support for the idea and the land from government officials, getting the money to fund the project was a different task altogether. Since the use of taxpayer money was virtually unheard of at the time, thousands of small donations, as well as corporate donations from notable companies such as US Steel and Sears, Roebuck & Company were obtained by Bess Sheehan from the Indiana Federation of Women's Clubs. By July 1, 1926, the park was fully funded and opened its gates to almost 63,000 visitors in its first three months of operation.

SAVE THE DUNES COUNCIL AND DOROTHY BUELL

Establishing the state park was just the beginning, however; the park and the surrounding area began to be loved to death as the dunes became a popular tourist attraction. Under the direction of Dorothy Buell, the Save the Dunes Council was born from the humble meetings at her home in Ogden Dunes in 1952. The group's main goal was to save more land and help preserve the parkland that had already been established. Due to their dedication and perseverance, the group grew from its small stature to a political and skillful task force that led the way to establishing the area into a national lakeshore. By the mid-1960s, the group had persuaded 22 groups to join their preservation cause, including the Hoosier Environmental Council, the National Audubon Society, and the Sierra Club. Together they were able to finally persuade Congress to authorize the Indiana Dunes National Lakeshore in late 1966, thus setting aside and protecting an additional 5,300 acres surrounding Indiana Dunes State Park. As time has progressed, additional land has been saved, and the group continues to fight the ecological destruction of the area today.

THE EFFECT OF INDUSTRIALIZATION

The 1960s proved to be a time of constant struggle for the dunes and those who were attempting to save them, as industrialization quickly expanded throughout the dunes area. A race to save the land from the industrial pressure of steel companies had begun and almost overnight steel companies, such as Bethlehem Steel and Midwest Steel, were buying up land and undertaking massive construction projects. Bethlehem Steel Corporation began one of the largest projects in the company's history,

Marram grass casts a shadow on the sandy dunes.

flattening the ancient landscape and filling marshes with 25,000 cubic yards of sand a day in order to build a million-square-foot foundation for its factory. While steel companies played a large role in the annihilation of the dunes, power companies, such as Northern Indiana Public Service Company (NIPSCO), also took on large-scale projects in order to supply the factories and the surrounding area with resources, such as free water used to produce electric power. While opposition by environmental groups only delayed construction, NIPSCO eventually succeeded in building two coal-fired power plants, a 345,000 kilowatt substation, a transmission line corridor, and facilities to support the massive power operations. The company's only loss came years later when attempting to build a nuclear plant, which was abandoned due to legal challenges, strong opposition, and an extravagant cost. By 1970, a three-mile long industrial corridor stretched the length of Lake Michigan's shoreline, forever changing the landscape while destroying the once natural beauty of the area.

Rife with wildlife, the tall, sandy dunes held tight with sparse vegetation and winding coastline, making the area a popular hot spot for birding. Near such a large body of water, many migrating birds stop in the area to rest while the thermal updrafts produced by the dunes make the perfect environment for incoming and outgoing flight patterns.

The park offers a nature center located near the campgrounds, with a display area, program room, library, live native animal display, and birdwatching room. Several loop trails located near the nature center lead into a nature preserve that makes up two-thirds of the park. Other features include an observation tower that overlooks the lake and a pavilion built in 1930.

Due to its unique landscape, Indiana Dunes offers explorers an opportunity to experience a blend of beach, bogs, and shaded woodlands almost simultaneously. However, due to the constant changing landscape, the park's trails and key features are often closed or damaged for various reasons for unknown amounts of time. The park's trails are currently numbered 2, 3, 4, 7, 8, 9, and 10, while once including Trails 1, 5, and 6. Over the years, Trail 1 was combined with Trail 3, creating its lower loop, which starts at the park office and main gate. Trails 5 and 6 no longer exist, and so much time has passed that employees do not know when and where they once occurred.

Parts of Trail 2, connecting to Trail 10 by way of a boardwalk, have been besieged by floodwater due to insatiable beaver activity. These and other fluctuations to the park, while seen as nuisances, are actually living proof of how uncontrollable the area actually is. For thousands of years the area has been in a constant change, and the ability to keep the state park functioning since the 1920s should be a witness to the hard work the staff of Indiana Dunes State Park has provided. Many of the shorter trails revolve around the three main dunes and key features of the park: Mt. Tom, Mt. Holden, and Mt. Jackson. Mt. Tom, named after Lieutenant Tom Brady, is made up of 56 million cubic feet of sand and stands 192 feet above Lake Michigan (771 feet above sea level), with a 43-degree slope. Mt. Holden, named after Charles Holden, the Prairie Club's first

Marram grass and other vegetation help hold the wind-swept dunes in place.

president, is made up of 53 million cubic feet of sand and stands 184 feet above Lake Michigan (763 feet above sea level) with a slope of 38 degrees. Mt. Jackson, named after Indiana Governor Edward Jackson, is made up of 32 million cubic feet of sand and stands 176 feet above Lake Michigan (755 feet above sea level) with a slope of 31 degrees. Key features of the park and on park maps are the blowouts, large depressions left from sediment, which are carved out of the dunes due to high wind. Beach House Blowout is actually a pair of blowouts separated by a forested dune that runs perpendicular with the lake. Furnessville Blowout is an open grassy and sandy field closed off from the lakeshore by a foredune. Big Blowout is a wide, open space looking very similar to rolling hills and valleys.

The twilight hours offer visitors a romantic view of Indiana Dunes State Park.

DUNES NATURE PRESERVE

Encompassing 1,530 acres, the preserve comprises the eastern two-thirds of Indiana Dunes State Park and protects the best natural features of the park. Small mats of bearberry (kinnikinnick), a procumbent evergreen shrub, add stability to the soil as beach grass with its spreading underground root system, and establish little islands of cover in the windblown sand. As the elevation increases, sumac, sand cherry, cottonwood, and prostrate juniper gradually take over the sandy shoreline. South of the dunes is a wetland area, composed of marsh, shrub swamp, and swamp forest.

DUNES PRAIRIE NATURE PRESERVE

The 58-acre tract of land is located in the southwest corner of Indiana Dunes State Park and contains a noteworthy prairie remnant that has been monitored by botanists for decades. It also contains a tributary of Dunes Creek, surrounded by a black oak savanna, swamp forest, and a dune covered in herbaceous graminoid grass features. Periodic prescribed burns keep these natural communities in a healthy condition. This preserve also contains outstanding prairie and a wide variety of native wildflowers.

TRAIL 2

(3 miles) Easy—The path begins near the southwest shelter, heading parallel with Dunes Creek, crossing the park road twice before entering Dunes Nature Preserve. The long stretch of trail is easily hiked and remains one of the best trails in the park for spring wildflowers and ferns. While heavily wooded and lush, the area is actually second-growth, lowland forest, clear-cut before the land was given to the park before the early 1920s. The trail has several wooden bridges crossing over wetland ditches. These crossings mark the spots at which an attempt was made at one time or another to drain the area for farming with little success. After the trail crosses the road near the Wilson Shelter, the forest changes from a once clear-cut landscape to trees that have lived half a century or longer as the path leads into Dunes Nature Preserve. While the trail is designed to continue heading east, reaching a wooden boardwalk that then heads north, the boardwalk area is often closed—submerged or unable to be crossed due to flooding caused by beavers. This flooded area has proved to be an expensive area to keep open, so the last leg of the path attaching to Trail 10 is almost always closed. Due to the terrain design, it is the perfect area for cross-country skiing during the winter months.

TRAIL 3

(0.75 miles) Moderate—This short path leads through Dune Prairie Nature Preserve in the most eastern section of Indiana Dunes State Park, providing the best opportunity to learn about forest succession within the dune landscape and ample opportunities to view late-blooming summer flowers and Indiana's native prickly pear cactus. The southern section of Trail 3 was once Trail 1, and it touches the south edge of a 10-acre area that a raging fire burned in 1969 before it could be contained.

TRAIL 4

(0.75 miles) Moderate—This trail connects the campground shelter with Trail 8 on top of Mt. Tom before heading back downhill by way of wooden steps leading to Trail 7 and the beach.

TRAIL 7

(1.1 miles) Moderate—The short path is a connector trail leading uphill to Trail 8, between Mt. Tom and Mt. Holden. It is primarily used as a shortcut back to the nature center for those who need a break from the

Three Dune Challenge. From the nature center, the path is also the most direct route to the beach.

TRAIL 8

(1.5 miles) Rugged—The path is the main trail to Indiana Dunes State Park's Three Dune Challenge, a rugged sandy trail boasted as the most difficult in the park. With some parts of the trail featuring a 40-degree slope, it can feel like every two steps forward results in a step back as sand begins to slide downhill around your feet. Accessible from the nature center or the pavilion and beach house, either direction results in climbing Mt. Tom, Mt. Holden, and Mt. Jackson.

TRAIL 9

(3.75 miles) Moderate—The path is a fine blend of forested dunes, intermittingly changing from full-sun, sandy dune tops to a shaded forest trail. The trail can be easily reached by one of the many spur trails leading from the beach or by either the western or central attachments to Trail 10. With the highest elevation of most of the longer trails, this path gives many opportunities to view the dunes and the beach from some of the park's higher points. The trail skirts the southern edge of the Beach House Blowout and the Furnessville Blowout.

TRAIL 10

(5.5 miles) Moderate—The trail begins at the pavilion and beach house along the western edge of the park's shore and follows along the shoreline, heading east for approximately 2.79 miles before reaching a mile marker leading south into the shaded woods. While following the shoreline, the trail passes six blowouts—Beach House Blowout, Furnessville Blowout, Big Blowout, and three smaller ones created by foot traffic and the changing of the lake's water levels. Traveling into the woods and uphill briefly, the path then follows a smooth trail through Dunes Nature Preserve. The trail is heavily forested and best represents what the forest would have originally looked like in pioneer times, passing a wide-open woodland named Paradise Valley and a stretch of pine trees known as the Pinery. The trail connects with Trail 9, by way of a spur trail, and passes the often-closed portion of Trail 2 and a long stretch of beautiful bogs before it reaches Trail 9 once again at the western end of the preserve.

5

Pokagon State Park

Established 1925—1,260 acres

450 Lane 100 Lake James

Angola, IN 46703

(260) 833-2012

41.713889, -85.025278

Pokagon State Park was initially called Lake James State Park but was changed to acknowledge the area's deep Native American heritage. The park's name honors Chief Leopold Pokagon, one of the last leaders of the Potawatomi tribe and his influential son, Simon—who was believed to be one of the most educated Native Americans of the time. Studying at Notre Dame, Simon spent most of his life working toward the betterment of his people, meeting with Abraham Lincoln twice to discuss tribal issues and land claims.

Before the property was a state park, the land was made up of several farmsteads. The rough terrain and sandy, rocky soil made farming extremely difficult but served perfectly for the site of a recreational facility. The idea of a state park in Steuben County first arose from a report by the Indiana Department of Conservation in 1923, mentioning an area containing over 500 acres known as Failing Estate. As local citizens began to learn of the possibility of a state park in their area, a campaign was devised to raise money for the property using a subscription of funds. The following year Richard Lieber spoke at an October meeting with the Steuben County Chamber of Commerce, suggesting the county was an acceptable place for a state park, and the chamber unanimously voted to establish a drive to raise money to purchase the property. In 1925, the Indiana legislature passed an act that allowed all counties to purchase property and turn ownership over to the state of Indiana to be managed as a park. After a successful fund drive to raise money for the property by issuing bonds, $35,000 was used toward the purchase of the property the same year. By 1926, the property once known as Lake James State Park had grown to 700 acres with the addition of two new tracts of land, and construction began on a park inn.

The park was given to the people of Indiana as a Christmas gift from Steuben County residents in December of 1925, with an official dedication ceremony the following July. Originally formed from 580 acres purchased from Thomas Failing, the property was then described as "a barren tract of land, devoid of scenic beauty." Today much has changed, as the old farmlands have been transformed back into a beautiful forested property consisting of 1,260 acres.

THE POTAWATOMI INN

The park's Potawatomi Inn takes its name from the Native American tribe who made their home in the area of the Great Plains. Construction began in 1926, and the architectural design was based on English Tudor style, using red brick and tile, stucco, and rough, exposed timber beams. As with many state park structures built during the same era, materials were mostly taken from the property, including the wood from downed trees and split stones to fashion the fireplaces and chimneys. The Potawatomi Inn welcomed the Lake James Cottage Owners Association as its first guests in May of 1927. The inn was officially dedicated on June 17, 1927, with the original 20-room facility costing $70,000 to construct. Around 1940 the alcove addition was completed, which included guest rooms on the second floor, a small dining room on the first floor, and a game room called the Pow Wow Room on a lower level. The Pow Wow Room was later converted into a banquet room called the Wig Wam Room. In 1950 individual restrooms were installed, and the carriage house was converted into motel rooms. The Hoosier Wing, an enormous two-story structure, was built in 1968, adding 16 guest rooms on the upper floor and a banquet room on the lower floor. During the 1980s a renovation of the interior took place, which added the inn's first elevator and an indoor swimming pool and sun deck in 1982. In March of 1994 a $7.5 million expansion added 59 rooms, 10,000 square feet of banquet space, and a new lobby. Dedication of the new construction occurred on

December 1, 1995. Today, the inn is host to 137 rooms, including four lavish cabin suites, a restaurant and Courtyard Café, a modest library, and eight meeting rooms of various sizes—all along the shore of beautiful Lake James.

CCC

Established during the time of the Civilian Conservation Corps (CCC), Pokagon State Park features the distinctive architecture and engineering of the era in all of its beautiful stone and log structures, including the inn, designed in an up-north fishing-lodge theme. Before being stationed at Pokagon State Park, the CCC trained at Fort Knox, Kentucky, and was first assigned to Indiana Dunes State Park. While residents of the Pokagon property, the CCC were responsible for building the swimming beaches, the saddle barn, the Spring Shelter, the beach bathhouse, the park office, and the campgrounds. Additionally, they constructed all of the roads, built retaining walls, did massive tree planting, and created the trails as well as the majority of the facilities still used today. The CCC Combination Shelter was built in 1936 and has long been the location for winter ski activities. The saddle barn was built in 1937 and continues to operate today as a horse rental facility. Constructed in 1937, the Spring Shelter is a small building located within the campground area and is the cornerstone location where many hikes originate. One of the most notable features in the park is the County Road Bridge, originally constructed by the CCC in 1936 before it was replaced by a cement bridge in 1953. In 2000, the cement bridge was rebuilt with a replica of the CCC's original wooden structure to honor the men's original architectural design. The CCC shelter was listed in 1992 on the National Register of Historic Places, and as of 1996, close to 1,000 acres of park property is listed on the National Register of Historic Places.

Between 1934 and 1942, CCC Company 556 was stationed at a temporary camp containing 12 buildings—memorialized today with an educational walking experience near the nature center. While the buildings were removed when the CCC left the property, trails through a grassy field lead visitors to 11 locations with wooden poles representing the four corners of each building. A map available from the nature center outlines the previous camp's design, which includes the locations of six barracks, a latrine, bathhouse, recreation hall, administration building, and mess hall. The latrine served as the camp's outhouse and was in four different locations while the camp was in operation. These four locations left depressions in the landscape that can still be seen today. Barracks 3 was the farthest from all of the camp's facilities but had the shortest walking distance to the toboggan slide. Barracks 4 was the noisiest since it sat in the middle of camp but had the best access to the camp's latrine late at night. Barracks 6 was once called "Barracks 13" or "Foreign Legion" because it housed the camp's troublemakers. The 18-by-26-foot bathhouse was shared by more than 180 men staying in the camp. The recreation hall was once named Weaver Hall in honor of a well-liked commanding officer. The hall offered men a post office, library, and billiards and ping-pong tables. The administration building housed the camp offices as well as the camp medical clinic and infirmary.

Roger Woodcock was a stonemason with Company 556 from 1936 to 1939, and after leaving the CCC he continued his love for masonry, building rock walls, fireplaces, and monuments around northeastern Indiana. He became a constant presence at Pokagon State Park, returning to teach rockwork to the staff as well as leading programs. The park has been host to annual CCC reunions for over 50 years; Roger played an important role in organizing these until his passing in 2007.

The original gatehouse at the park's entrance was built in 1936 and served the park to collect entrance fees until 1989 when a new gatehouse was constructed in the center of the road. The original gatehouse has since been converted into a small museum, briefly describing the property's history and CCC involvement. It is here that visitors can learn about how the park's masonry work was constructed using a distinct type of stone brought to the area from Canada by prehistoric glaciers. It was common during the era of the CCC to take a glacial boulder the size of a desk and break it down into manageable pieces to be used as puzzle pieces for constructing fireplaces and other stone structures. The group's goal was to have mortar joints no wider than three-quarters of an inch, which took an impressive amount of patience and skill. It is because of the hard work by CCC masons that the buildings constructed for the park will remain permanent fixtures.

THE LAKES

Steuben County, where Pokagon State Park resides, has more lakes than any other county in Indiana, with a total of 120. These lakes are evidence of the Wisconsinan glaciation that moved through the area and halted during the last ice age. The gouging and piling of the earth's surface by the mighty ice created varying depths and designs of the lakes, which

Lake James and Snow Lake form an attractive background to Pokagon State Park and provide ample opportunities for water sports.

make the area even more unique. During the era of the Potawatomi Indians, the lakes were a part of an enormous swamp used by the Natives for hunting grounds. Pokagon State Park is surrounded by two major lakes on its north, west, and south borders—Lake James and Snow Lake. Other lakes off property that are connected to the waters of Pokagon State Park include Jimmerson Lake to the west and Otter Lakes to the east.

Lake James is divided into three sections, the Upper, Middle, and Lower Basins. An old atlas states that Lake James was named by pioneer surveyor James Watson Riley, but it is speculated that the lake was named by another person in Riley's honor. Indiana's fourth largest lake, Lake James has a surface area of about 1,229 acres and roughly 17.5 miles of shoreline. With the exception of Pokagon State Park, most of the shoreline has been developed with private cottages and campgrounds dating back over 100 years. The lakes of the area were first surveyed in 1831 by E. H. Lytle. This first survey once considered Snow Lake a fourth section of Lake James before vegetation eventually separated the two lakes around the end of the 1800s.

DRYER HILL

Dryer Hill was dedicated by the Indiana Department of Conservation to the memory of Charles Redaway Dryer, who loved the lakes and hills according to his report on the region to the state geological survey in 1891. A memorial rock with a plaque is located near the toboggan slides in a once popular area for sledding prior to the construction of the toboggan run.

TOBOGGAN WARMING CENTER

One of only two facilities of its kind, the toboggan run was originally a single track built in 1935 by the CCC for their own personal use. The original track had curves similar to a bobsled course but was straightened in 1936 to increase speed. Today there are two tracks that are a major attraction in the winter months; sleds reach speeds of over 40 miles per hour. The 30-foot tower replaced an old platform in 1974, and the tracks became refrigerated, making cold weather and ice unnecessary. Prior to refrigerating the tracks, ice blocks were cut from Lake James and carved to fit the tracks. The quarter-mile track includes a 90-foot vertical drop and an approximate ride time of 30 seconds.

CROSS-COUNTRY SKIING

The CCC Combination Shelter located near the upper basin of Lake James provides ski rentals, even for people with little to no experience. Since Pokagon's northern location makes it a perfect destination for winter activities, ski rental has historically been a staple. The park offers three ski trails of variable skill levels, which include a beginner, a moderate, and an advanced-rugged loop.

POTAWATOMI NATURE PRESERVE

Located in the eastern section of Pokagon State Park, the Potawatomi Nature Preserve is a 256-acre property consisting of the natural Lake Lonidaw, named in honor of Simon Pokagon's wife. Other features include cattail marshes, sedge meadows, tamarack and yellow birch swamps, and adjoining uplands covered with hardwoods. Historically known as an outstanding example of the original landscape that once existed in the Northeastern Morainal Lake Region, the higher ridges of the preserve support stands of red oak, white oak, wild black cherry, shagbark hickory, and sugar maple.

Red-stem dogwoods brighten the winter woods with colorful hues.

BEECHWOOD NATURE PRESERVE

Located near the northeast edge of the park, the Beechwood Nature Preserve is off park property but accessed from Trail 8. The 89-acre property has a 1.5-mile-loop trail that passes over rolling hills and through old meadows, which are the remnants of an old apple orchard. Named for the blue beech trees that are scattered on the property, a boardwalk also allows visitors to pass through a lowland swamp that features rare yellow birch, red maple, red elm, and skunk cabbage. A part of ACRES Land Trust, the property was donated by two sisters, Mildred and Garnette Foster, in 1964. Memorial trees were planted for both sisters after they passed away—an oak tree for Mildred who died in 1988 and a sugar maple for Garnette who died in 1991.

The park offers five shelters, including the CCC Combination Shelter, which is divided into two separate spaces, and the Apple Orchard Shelter, Sweet Gum Shelter, and Black Cherry Shelter. The park also offers a

THE COMPLETE GUIDE TO INDIANA STATE PARKS

Originally started by two young men, the toboggan slide at Pokagon State Park has become a world-class winter experience.

The trails are lined with the spring color of redbud trees.

nature center with an exhibit room, where guests are greeted by the park staff who regularly lead interpretive programs.

CAMPGROUNDS

The original campground built by the CCC is the smallest on the property and is now known as Campground 1. The number of campsites once grew to 435, until 160 campsites were removed to ease noise pollution for park guests. Today, Pokagon State Park offers 200 campsites with electric and 73 nonelectric sites, divided into five distinct campgrounds. A swimming beach is located nearby and plenty of hiking trails give visitors access to the central part of the park. Also in the middle of the campground is an amphitheater, primarily used during summer holiday weekends for campfire programs.

The group camp area, built in the 1930s by the CCC, was once known as the Pokagon Boys Camp. A business partnership was arranged between camp leader and former Olympic athlete Hermon Phillips and the park, to operate the camp during the summer as a place for boys to go to learn outdoor skills. The camp operated until the 1960s along with a similar girls' camp on the opposite side of the lake, also owned by Phillips. When the boys' camp was closed, the buildings were turned over to the state and used by the park for group camping. Keeping with the Native American theme, the name was changed to Camp Mitig, meaning "a meeting place in the woods." Two former campers that attended Pokagon Boys Camp in 1948 and 1949, Donald Hughes and Evans Rust, set up a preservation fund with Steuben County in 2006. Hughes also released a documentary film about his time at the camp called *An American Boy*. Today the camp is well-preserved, containing a kitchen/dining hall, counselor's cabin, north and south bunkhouses, 11 cabins that sleep eight, and a modern shower building.

During the warmer months, the park offers endless opportunities for boating, fishing, and swimming but is also a popular place to take a hike. Pokagon State Park offers visitors nine hiking trails from easy to rugged as well as a horse trail connected to the park's saddle barn.

TRAIL 1

(2 miles) Moderate—The trail is a series of looping paths that connect the Potawatomi Inn, nature center, and saddle barn to the southwestern section of the park. While passing through hardwood forests, the trail crosses a bridge at the park road and is a good trail for birding and wildflowers.

TRAIL 2

(2.2 miles) Moderate—The trail can be accessed near the gatehouse and is a shared path, also used as a horse trail. The trail connects with Trail 3 along its eastern section and leads past the campgrounds, making a loop back once reaching the park's northwestern tip near Snow Lake.

TRAIL 3

(2.2 miles) Moderate—The long loop trail leads through portions of the Potawatomi Nature Preserve and gives visitors access to Lake Lonidaw. The northeastern section of the trail leads to a panoramic overlook called Hell's Point just between the park's border and the Beechwood Nature Preserve property owned by ACRES Land Trust. The name is in reference to a preacher who once held a revival near the location and, when disappointed with the outcome of the revival meetings, said the area was a "regular hell's point." While the reference wasn't intended to describe the specific location we know today, locals over time simply designated the overlook as Hell's Point.

TRAIL 4

(1.4 miles) Easy—The trail is a connection path that begins near the gatehouse along the same route used for Trail 2 and leads to the amphitheater, through the campgrounds. The path leads through a variety of habitats, including hardwood forests and evergreens.

TRAIL 5

(0.7 miles) Easy—The trail leads north to south connecting Campground 1 and the group camp area to the Lake James Bath House & Beach. The trail is also a good trail for birding and wildflowers.

TRAIL 6

(0.7 miles) Moderate—The trail is accessed at two locations from Trail 3 and leads through the southeastern section of the park. The path loops through one of the more primitive sections and leads through a swamp containing marshland trees, plants, and wildlife.

TRAIL 7

(1.8 miles) Moderate—Known as the Bluebird Hills Trail, the path begins east of Trail 3 and Hell's Point, leading through a central portion of the Potawatomi Nature Preserve. A long stretch of straight path leads to a loop that traverses a secluded wetland. The trail is mostly grasslands and an environmental experience that was typical of the land prior to farming.

TRAIL 8

(1 mile) Moderate—The trail is accessed from Trail 3 in its southern section and connects with Trail 7 in the northwest with a loop trail in the center of those two points. The trail is one of the newest to the park and traverses open hills and meadows. This trail was designed to give park visitors access to ACRES Land Trust Beechwood Nature Preserve.

TRAIL 9

(1.7 miles) Rugged—Accessed from Trail 3, the path leads southeast into the eastern portion of the Potawatomi Nature Preserve, looping back at the park's eastern border. The path is the park's only rugged trail and leads visitors through wooded swamps, passing stone dams built by the CCC and near the old site of the Pokagon Motel that once operated where the park border reaches Indiana 127.

6

Spring Mill State Park

Established 1927—1,358 acres

3333 State Road 60 E.

Mitchell, IN 47446

(812) 849-3534

38.733333, -86.42

The story of the Spring Mill property first began in 1814 when Ensign Samuel Jackson, a Canadian-born US Navy officer, and his wife first moved into the area, building a cabin and gristmill near what is known today as Hamer Cave. Having served as a guide through the Indiana Territory for General William Henry Harrison, Jackson was familiar with the wilderness, particularly the flowing cave water that could supply power to a mill. With no real deed to the property, Jackson depended on "squatter's rights" in order to live and work on the land for two years until receiving an official patent for three tracts of land in 1816. Surprisingly, with no explanation, the couple sold their humble estate of land, buildings, gardens, an orchard, and woods and moved back to Columbia County, Pennsylvania, only five months after they received the land patent.

With development already in place, the land was sold to two major landowners, brothers named Cuthbert and Thomas Bullitt. Famed in promoting wilderness communities, the two, known as "The Merchants of Louisville," bought vast land tracts in southern Indiana and Kentucky, ruling over their wilderness properties from the comfort of their riverside mansions in what is now the riverfront and business district of

A restored three-story limestone gristmill, built in 1817, still grinds cornmeal today.

downtown Louisville, Kentucky. Samuel's original gristmill was replaced with the current three story stone-walled mill, an enormous water wheel, and the long, raised flume made of tulip poplar, wrought iron, and limestone piers. Given the time period, it was a remarkable task by many skilled professionals to finish the large-scale mill in only six months, ready for operation by the autumn months of 1817. A man named Uriah Glover was hired to supervise the construction and manage the gristmill.

An industrial pioneer village dating back to the 1800s offers visitors a view of life in the past.

For a wilderness operation, the enterprise was very successful almost overnight. More buildings were constructed, including mansion-like cabins for Glover and his family as well as the Bullitt brothers. Interested more in the development of the property than actually running a mill despite its success, the Bullitt brothers sold their stock in the village for $20,000 in one day—a small fortune for the time period. The mill, the two large homes, and 1,440 acres of land were sold to William and Joseph Montgomery. Also brothers of business wealth, the Montgomerys added an additional sawmill, a tavern, and a distillery with many more plans of growth. Further plans for development ceased, however, in 1827 when Joseph Montgomery died. After his brother William died five years later, the village was sold once again by William's son for a mere $7,000 on June 11, 1832, to Hugh and Thomas Hamer. For the third time the village was owned by two brothers, and the best years of the village were just around the corner. Not strangers of the area, the two brothers were actually well trained millwrights working for the former owners since 1825. As

Native stone was used to build many inspiring architectural designs within Spring Mill State Park's pioneer village and garden.

the new owners, the brothers and their families moved into the beautiful residences built for the Bullitt brothers and Uriah Glover. While business had always been good, it picked up more than ever, and Hugh Hamer financed a remodel of their homes and built a schoolhouse for the village children. The hustle and bustle of the town had increased so much that farmers would have to wait almost 10 days in peak season to get their corn ground. They in turn often paid the Hamers in corn instead of money, which was distilled into whiskey and sold in the tavern. While at its peak between 1840 and 1850, the tavern became a regular stop for stagecoaches traveling from Louisville to Terre Haute. Spring Mill soon became epic in trade, exporting their goods by way of the White River, just north of the town.

With the development of railroads through the area between 1853 and 1857, Spring Mill began to lose its fame because the construction of the rail line bypassed the village without a stop. When a new line was constructed nearby, a train station was built at a crossing point of tracks known as Mitchell Crossing—today the location of the nearby town of Mitchell. When many of the village residents moved to Mitchell to be near the newly constructed railroad, the village's property value was cut in half, to a mere $15,000. When Hugh Hamer died on March 10, 1872, of smallpox, his son Robert sold the property at a major loss to a man by the name of Jonathan Turley. Changing the name to Daisy Spring Mill, Turley upgraded and modernized the facilities to better match operations of the time. Although he boosted the production of spirits and was once known to have the best brandy in the Midwest, the operation still failed to make adequate profits, and Turley closed the mill in 1892 and later the distillery in 1896. Turley died later that same year.

With all hope of revitalizing the village now gone, focus was turned to the neighbors of the village who had begun to develop their own properties. James C. Lynn owned and operated a sawmill on 445 acres near what is now known as Donaldson Cave. Although his business was successful, a strange man with a Scottish accent talked the man out of his entire property in 1865 for $3,500. The eccentric, wealthy man was George Donaldson. A lover of nature, Donaldson bought the property for the sole reason of preserving the land and all of the flora and fauna that called the land home, a very odd act at the time. As an avid naturalist, Donaldson protected every animal and plant on his newly purchased property, allowing no hunting or timber production whatsoever. His preservation led to his forest remaining virgin timber even today, now protected by the Donaldson Woods Nature Preserve. He moved away to Alabama in 1882 because his house, known as Shawnee Cottage, was robbed and burned to the ground, and he never returned. Choosing to live out his last days in Scotland, he never returned to the property and died in 1898. Since Donaldson did not have a will, his land's ownership underwent years of legal battles with two fundamental supreme court cases. Ownership of the land was eventually given to Indiana University in 1915 when the university was able to buy the property for $4,000. The establishment of Spring Mill State Park began around 1927 when Indiana University made the decision to give 183 acres of the Donaldson tract to the State Department of Conservation in an effort to add to the state's new state park system. As part of the deal with the university's gift, an additional 539 acres west of the Donaldson tract would need to be acquired by the county and attached.

While a portion of Turley's property remained in the family, what remained of the decaying village and almost 300 acres was bought by the

Lehigh Portland Cement Company in the town of Mitchell. While they had no interest in the village, what they really wanted was exactly what drew Samuel Jackson to the property almost 100 years prior—the cold water supply, which held a constant temperature above freezing, rushing from the cave. This water was used to cool lime kilns for the commercial production of lime (calcium oxide). Once Richard Lieber became aware of the old village, he envisioned its restoration and knew it had to be a part of the park. Lieber explained his idea to Harry Trexler, the chairman of the Lehigh Portland Cement Company, and Trexler became so enthusiastic about the idea of adding the property and restoring the village that he sold the entire tract of land and the village to Richard Lieber and the state of Indiana for a single dollar—with the agreement that the cement company would continue to own the water rights.

With the help of Elam Y. Guerney, a local historian and the park's first superintendent, Richard Lieber and a team of individuals restored the village to its present-day condition. The 24-foot, 8-ton water wheel proved to be the hardest of the reconstruction projects, since not many engineers had the knowledge of how to build such a device with historic accuracy. With Denzil Doggett and Oren Reed at the helm of project engineering, a team with as many as 20 men at times was able to accurately build the wheel in 11 weeks, using discovered relic wheel parts and a book written by a millwright from the 1800s. The wheel was completed on October 18, 1931. The original grinding stones for the mill, which had been brought from France by the Bullitt brothers, had been found mostly buried and in tall weeds. The grinding stones were installed and used until April 1962. Once the grinding stones finally wore out, they were replaced with granite stones from North Carolina. While Hugh Hamer's springhouse, nursery, and other structures were restored around 1933, several buildings that were not originally on the property were also brought in for preservation purposes. These include the Granny White house, home of famed area pioneer woman Sallie Cummins White, as well as The Sheeks house, which was built in 1816 and originally located three miles from the village property.

Before his death in 1896, Jonathan Turley was also in the business of the commercial production of lime. Two abandoned lime kilns still exist on the property, near Mill Creek Bridge and the other in the village. While much of the property fell into decay and faded back into the forest property, Turley's home remained standing until 1950 when it had to be torn down due to ill repair, and his barns and fields were converted into what is now the campground area. Turley's property was donated to the park in 1934 by his daughter Eliza, in honor of her father.

CCC

The Civilian Conservation Corps (CCC) Company 1536 arrived at Spring Mill State Park around 1933, taking the lead role in building fences, trails, picnic areas, and the shelters, and they restored the Thomas Hamer house in the village in 1935. Additionally, the CCC is responsible for the creation of Spring Mill Lake by building dams to contain the flowing waters from two major cave systems. The crew stayed and worked on the property until 1940.

CAVES

Located on the Mitchell Karst Plain, the area is rife with caves and sink-holes due to the large collection of limestone. Bronson Cave, Twin Caves, Donaldson Cave, and Hamer Cave exist and have been the focal point for locals dating back to the 1800s. The openings of Bronson Cave were created by a roof collapse, and the cave gets its name from a local resident who lived in the area in the 1860s. The Twin Caves (Upper and Lower) were once the same structure until an ancient roof collapse opened the tunnel to the way we see it today. The cave once known as Shawnee Cave in Donaldson's era was later changed to Donaldson Cave to honor the man who once protected its entry. Donaldson Cave connects Bronson Cave with the Twin Caves and was once the site of historic research on the famed blind cave fish by Indiana University biologist Dr. Carl H. Eigenmann (1863–1927). Hamer Cave is of particular importance, as water rushing from its inner stream has powered the gristmills on the property since 1814 and continues to do so today. First used by Samuel Jackson, the cave is named for the Hamer brothers who once owned the Pioneer Village where the current operational gristmill sits.

SPRING MILL INN

Set amid a backdrop of forest hills is Spring Mill Inn, built between 1936 and 1939 using native limestone. The beginning stages of the foundation and stone walls were constructed by the CCC Company 1536 and were finished by the Works Progress Administration (WPA) workers in 1938, under the supervision of engineers Henry H. Morgan and Henry Prange. Several obstacles plagued the project, including financial issues that kept the inn from being built as it was originally designed—deleting an east

Built in the late 1930s, Spring Mill Inn remains one of the main focal points for vacationers in southern Indiana.

wing from the construction. When the state of Indiana sold massive quantities of sand to the city of Chicago for its world's fair, the money from the sale was directed to the building of Spring Mill Inn. With the CCC and WPA foundation already in place and the money acquired to finish the project, Whittenburg Construction Company from Louisville, Kentucky, was awarded the task of finishing the Spring Mill Inn Project. Further obstacles arose during construction when a cave was discovered underneath the inn. In order to support the enormous building safely, concrete pilings had to be constructed to hold the building over a 15-by-29-foot cavernous hole.

Completed in 1939, the inn appointed its first manager, Myron L. Rees, with an official dedication ceremony of the inn on July 6, 1939. In the remaining months of its first year open, 8,000 guests registered and stayed overnight at the inn, with attendance to the park reaching 189,000.

Cooling the inn proved to be an obstacle, with early consideration of using the cold air from Donaldson Cave to cool the massive building. While the idea never happened, the inn went without any form of air conditioning until the 1960s. Today, the inn remains essentially the same as it did when it was completed, aside from a major renovation in 1976, which added 29 sleeping rooms and the east wing originally deleted from the project. The historic 73-room inn is warm and cozy with country decor, yet it offers modern-day accommodations like a conference room and an indoor/outdoor pool.

The park offers a multitude of educational experiences through three other interpretive facilities, including a nature center overlooking Spring Mill Lake, Grissom Memorial honoring Hoosier astronaut Virgil Grissom, and the Twin Caves Boat Tour, which highlights cave formations and cave creatures.

LAKEVIEW ACTIVITY CENTER

Costing $35,000 to build, this nature center was originally used as the park's first bathhouse and bathing beach; it was converted to an interpretive educational center in 1985.

GRISSOM MEMORIAL

Born on April 3, 1926, Virgil I. Grissom's boyhood home is located just up the road in the little town of Mitchell, near the corner of Grissom Avenue and Seventh Street. Moving into the home in 1927, Grissom was raised in the area in the same house until graduating high school in 1944. The house continued to be owned by the family until the mid-1990s when the property was sold and maintained by Virgil I. Grissom, Inc.

The Virgil I. Grissom Memorial stands as a monument to the man that made several notable historic endeavors while employed as a US astronaut. After graduating high school, Grissom enlisted to fight in World War II and used the GI bill to attend Purdue University, gaining a degree in mechanical engineering in February 1950. After joining the US Air Force, Grissom was shipped overseas to fight in the Korean War. Upon his return, Grissom worked for the Air Force Institute of Technology in Ohio and Edwards Air Force Base in California, logging a stunning 4,600 hours as a jet pilot. Grissom's astronaut career began in 1959 when the National Air and Space Administration (NASA) announced Virgil as one of the country's first seven astronauts for the Mercury 7 project. Grissom became America's second man in space on July 21, 1961, in a capsule known as "Liberty Bell 7." Flying nearly 81,000 miles in three orbits around the earth, Grissom made history again on March 23, 1965, during the Gemini III mission, when he became the first person to ever control and change the path of a spacecraft while in orbit. During a prelaunch test on the Apollo I mission in January 1967, Grissom was suddenly killed during a horrible fire in the command module, alongside fellow astronauts Ed White and Roger Chaffee, at Cape Kennedy, known today as Cape Canaveral Air Force Station. Virgil I. "Gus" Grissom was buried at Arlington National Cemetery, and the Indiana Department of Natural Resources sought to immediately recognize Grissom in memorial, building the museum and officially dedicating it on July 21, 1971.

TWIN CAVES BOAT TOUR

The Twin Caves Boat Tour first began enthralling visitors in 1937. Today, the 30-minute guided boat tour offers visitors an up-close encounter with the park's underground geology, streams, and sinkholes that connect the outside world to the cave below. Viewing rare animal life such as blind crayfish is a key feature of the subterranean experience. Cave tours operate from Memorial Day to October, and you can register the day of the trip.

The campground features 188 Class A campsites that include 30-amp electric service, a fire ring, and a picnic table for each site. Thirty-five primitive campsites and youth camping are also available. Four "comfort stations" are located in the campground, which include modern plumbing, restrooms, and showers. A camp store is accessible from both inside and outside the campground.

Six rentable shelters are available, located in every one of the most popular areas of the park: Oak Ridge Shelter, Tulip Poplar Shelter, Butternut Shelter, Donaldson Shelter, Pine Hill Shelter, and Sycamore Shelter.

HAMER CAVE

The showcase of the Pioneer Village is the gristmill. This limestone mill, an original structure that was built in 1817, still grinds corn to this day. Water flowing out of Hamer Cave pours over the enormous water wheel and drives the gears that spin the grindstones.

MITCHELL KARST PLAINS NATURE PRESERVE

The 459-acre tract is a classic example of karst terrain consisting of a very pronounced sinkhole plain that borders the entrenched valley of Mill Creek. The area is dominated by an abundance of sinkholes in various states of activity; many quickly swallow rainwater, whereas others are plugged and remain ponded for short time periods. The natural opening and collapse of small caverns throughout exemplify the very dynamic nature of this landscape. This portion of Spring Mill appears to represent the largest single block of undisturbed sinkhole plain in a natural forest community remaining in Indiana.

DONALDSON CAVE/WOODS NATURE PRESERVE

Made up of a 39-acre cave preserve and a 145-acre woods preserve, the tract of land located in the central and southern section of Spring Mill State Park contains virgin timber and one of the last stands of old-growth forest left in the state. Believed to be one of the most picturesque locations in the state, the forest of the preserve is classified as a western mesophytic forest type, intermediate between beech-maple and oak-hickory tree types. An unusual feature of the woods is the high percentage of white oaks, as much of the water runoff from the forest drains through sinkholes, rather than surface streams.

TRAIL 1

(0.375 miles) Moderate—This trail begins at the inn and leads downhill to Spring Mill Lake, making a loop back uphill ending at the inn.

TRAIL 2

(0.5 miles) Moderate—The short one-way path connects the Lakeview Activity Center to the parking area for the Pioneer Village.

TRAIL 3

(2.5 miles) Rugged—The trail begins at the Donaldson Picnic Area, leading down to Donaldson Cave. Once past Donaldson Cave, the trail leads past a group of sinkholes while walking through the virgin timber forest of Donaldson Woods Nature Preserve. The trail passes Twin Caves and Bronson Cave before returning to the parking area.

TRAIL 4

(2 miles) Rugged—As an amateur bird enthusiast, George Donaldson was an admirer of the famed ornithologist and fellow Scotsman Alexander Wilson. Wilson having died in 1813, the two never actually met, yet Donaldson erected a monument in Wilson's honor in 1866 on his property near the streamed of what has become Trail 4, a short walk from the Spring Mill Inn. Passing many important features of the park, the trail is the best way to easily access the Wilson Monument, Donaldson Cave, the Hamer Pioneer Cemetery, Hamer Cave, and the Pioneer Village.

TRAIL 5
(1 mile) Moderate—This trail is the best way to see every angle of Spring Mill Lake, climbing rocky wetland banks and crossing over a picturesque waterfall draining from the north end of the lake.

TRAIL 6—GRISSOM MEMORIAL TRAIL
(0.25 miles) Accessible—The trail is a wide, paved path accessible by everyone; it begins at the front entrance of the parking area and loops around the backside of the Virgil I. Grissom Memorial.

TRAIL 7
(1.75 miles) Easy—The trail loops through and around Oak Ridge Picnic Area and connects with Trail 4 between the Hamer Cemetery and village.

STAGE COACH TRAIL
(0.5 miles) Moderate—The trail follows an old roadbed from the Pioneer Village to the Oak Ridge Picnic Area and Playground. The trail is a slightly rugged path with a steep incline.

MOUNTAIN BIKE TRAIL
(2 miles) Beginner—The dirt path leads north, located directly between Spring Mill Lake and the campground. The trail is a skinny loop, traveling through some of the park's best areas for a truly unique mountain biking experience. An easy path for biking, the trail is designed for beginners.

7

Shakamak State Park

Established 1928—1,766 acres

6265 W. State Road 48

Jasonville, IN 47438

(812) 665-2158

39.1771, -87.2329

The area surrounding what is now Shakamak State Park was once known as Golden Knobs; the land now under the man-made lake was known as Johnson Hollow. In the early 1900s as railroad construction reached the town of Jasonville, coal was discovered inside what would eventually be the park's boundaries. Two coal companies were quick to set up efficient operations—the Black Hawk Mine area and Golden Knob Mine. After years of working the land, coal production finally exhausted in the area around 1913, leaving the land undeveloped until the state park trend became a viable option for the used strip mine.

The idea for a state park first started around 1926 when a letter was written to the superintendent of Fisheries and Game of Indiana, George Mannfield. The letter proposed the idea of damming a five-foot culvert buried in an old railroad grade in order to create one of the largest lakes in the area at the time, Lake Shakamak. After years of planning and debate, the property needed was eventually purchased using money received from county-sold bonds. Dedicated on Labor Day, September 3, 1928, the park was originally called Tri-County State Park, honoring Clay, Greene, and Sullivan Counties for giving the state the land. By 1929, after extensive research was done on the preexisting railroad grade for use as

The buildings at Shakamak State Park are historical remnants of the talented mason workers from the past.

a dam, the culvert was blocked and water began to fill, completely covering Johnson Hollow. It's estimated that, at its completion, the lake was stocked with 40,000 bass, bluegill, and crappie. The same year, the name was officially changed to Shakamak State Park, referencing the Kickapoo Indiana word meaning long fish or eel. While fresh water eels do not exist in the lakes due to the dams, the nearby Wabash and Eel rivers are hot spots to find what the Native Americans considered a delicacy.

Development of the park was done by the Civilian Conservation Corps (CCC) Company 522. While on the property, the group replanted large portions of clear-cut land used during the days of mining, reforesting 300 acres while also landscaping five acres. Other tasks included building roads like the one that circles the entire boundary of Lake Shakamak, creating two miles of hiking trails, and building many of the structures that still exist today. The gatehouse, a saddle barn, the pool shelter, and many of the picnic shelters were constructed by the CCC using brick that was readily available at the time. Aside from coal mining, the area was also very well-known for brick manufacturing, which led to the buildings of Shakamak State Park being made almost entirely out of red brick instead of limestone like the majority of the other state parks. Beautiful brick structures were constructed, which remain almost like new today. Stretching from these buildings are long pathways of red brick, leading to parking areas and down brick stairways to the water's edge of the lake. Tragedy struck the CCC camp in the mid-1930s when a 19-year-old CCC worker named Theodore Grzbacz drowned in the lake while attempting to swim from the north finger of the lake, to the lake's shelter house, and then to the public beach—a distance of 150 feet. While swimming

with a companion named Flowers, the boy began having trouble just 15 yards from the destination, nearly drowning his friend Flowers as he attempted to help. After safely getting to shore, Flowers notified authorities, and when the boy could not be immediately found a search ensued stretching late into the night. The boy's body was eventually found in 25-foot-deep water using drag hooks in a section of the lake where large logs and debris still existed from the lake's creation. This was to be the first drowning at Shakamak State Park, setting a precedent for water safety and signaling an age of tighter restrictions.

A second lake was constructed not long after the CCC arrived on site, engineered by Garrett Schloot and Willard Humphreys. Using workers from another Roosevelt organization, the Civil Works Administration (CWA) constructed Lake Lenape using 137 men, 26 teams of horses, and eight trucks. When the CWA project ended before the lake could be completed, another federal agency called the Federal Emergency Relief Administration was called in to complete the work.

The third lake, Lake Kickapoo, was created in 1969 from the drainage of Lake Shakamak and Lake Lenape. Since the first two lakes are sub-impoundments, they help protect the water quality of Lake Kickapoo by trapping and filtering the water before it enters.

A particularly fascinating feature in the park that no longer exists was a 32-foot diving tower installed on the water's edge of Lake Shakamak. Between 1934 and the 1950s, Olympic trials and national swim meets were held at the park. In order to provide the necessary facilities, the park installed a large swimming platform, regulation-length swimming lanes, and the diving tower. These improvements allowed the park to host the Olympic swim trial in 1938. Throughout the 1930s, many of the swimmers who competed at Lake Shakamak went on to become famous Hollywood stars, since their roles often called for the actors to have athletic abilities or healthy physiques. A swimming and diving champion as a teenager, Esther Williams trialed for the Olympics before her dreams as an Olympic swimmer ended when World War II canceled two consecutive Olympics. She later appeared in a long list of Hollywood movies, many of which featured her in elaborate synchronized swimming routines. The 1932 gold medalist Buster Crabbe, best known for playing Flash Gordon and Buck Rogers with Universal Studios, participated in many events at the park—as did Johnny Weissmuller, one of the most famous actors to play the role of Tarzan.

POOL

As time passed, Lake Shakamak was eventually deemed unsafe for swimming due to the number of beach rescues by lifeguards and several more incidents of drowning. Located adjacent to the nature center and very close to the original swim beach, a fully updated family aquatic center was built to provide visitors a much-desired swimming outlet. The same beach house, locker rooms, and concessions that were used for the original swimming beach still exist and provide the aquatic center all of its necessary facilities. The pool features a 210-foot waterslide and an additional 12-foot slide for smaller kids.

Aside from swimming, Shakamak's main attraction continues to be its excellent fishing, along with paddle boating and row boating. The park offers group camping, cabins, and campsite rentals with all of the campsites in a wooded area—offering cool shade in the summer and beautiful fall colors in autumn. Amenities include tennis and basketball courts, three picnic shelters (Lenape, Tulip, and West), and a nature center offering free wildlife activities and nature hikes. The park is located approximately three miles from Jasonville, Indiana, a town with the motto of "The Gateway to Shakamak."

SHAKAMAK PRAIRIE NATURE PRESERVE

Established in 2012, the nature preserve is located along the west edge of the property. The 27.3-acre tract protects an example of prairie grassland in the Glaciated Section of the Southwestern Lowlands Natural Region. The nature preserve hosts a mesic prairie, the only protected example of

Brick architecture is a key feature of most of the older structures at Shakamak State Park.

a prairie natural community type in this entire natural region. Although it is believed that in presettlement times the Southwestern Lowlands Natural Region contained the greatest amount of prairie south of the Wisconsinan glacial border, most of the prairie has long been lost, making what can be protected in the preserve an especially important collection of prairie acreage.

CAMPGROUNDS

Located on the south side of Lake Lenape are 114 electric sites, 8 AA sites, 10 electric Maple Loop sites, and 43 primitive sites nestled in thick woodlands, providing shade and cover from the elements. While the campsites are very close, thick trees and the maturity of the forest provide a great deal of privacy from one site to the next. Electric RV sites 32 through 38 have the best view of the lake. A youth tent area is also located in the

Three man-made lakes at Shakamak
State Park offer 400 acres of water
for fishing and boating.

Spring-blooming dogwoods at Shakamak State Park.

northeast corner of the park, providing space for 120 young campers. A group camp for larger events is located along the edge of a northeast inlet of Lake Shakamak. The group camp can accommodate up to 270 campers and has dormitories, restrooms with showers, and a kitchen with dining hall.

CABINS
Shakamak State Park has an enormous collection of cabins within its border, 29 in all, which is more than any other state park in Indiana.

Beech trees light up the autumn woods with color.

Lakeview Cabins A and B are located on the west side of Lake Shakamak along with the majority of the cabins in the park. Cabins B, C, and D are located between the group camp and the youth camp and provide more facilities, such as running water, electric, and heat. There are also seven Rent-A-Camp cabins located in the campground.

TRAIL 1

(3.95 miles) Moderate—The path travels entirely around Lake Shakamak with some portions along the shoreline. It can be accessed at the nature center, near the cabins on the west side of Lake Shakamak, or near the group camp area.

TRAIL 2

(1.5 miles) Moderate—Evidence of the coal industry is present along this trail with a reconstructed mine entrance to Blackhawk mine. It accesses Trail 1 on the east side of Lake Shakamak and loops around the youth camp area and Cabins B, C, and D in the northeastern section of the park.

TRAIL 3

(1.4 miles) Moderate—The trail begins at the Lenape Shelter and leads north, crossing the park's roads several times before looping back south to the Lenape Shelter. The eastern section of the trail accesses Trail 4.

TRAIL 4

(1.6 miles) Moderate—A collection of bridges and stairs set the trail apart from the others. Beginning at the main campground, the trail leads east, north, and then west around Lake Lenape before meeting with Trail 3.

TRAIL 5

(2.20 miles) Moderate—This trail takes you along the shore of Lake Kickapoo. It is a great place for birdwatching.

TRAIL 6

(1.08 miles) Easy—This trail, which winds through forests of oak and pine, is used for both hiking and biking.

TRAIL 7

(1.60 miles) Easy—Similar to trail 6, this multiuse trail is also for hiking and biking. It is an excellent place to look for white-tailed deer.

8

Brown County State Park

Established 1929—15,815 acres

Nashville, IN 47448

(812) 988-6406

West Gate—1405 State Hwy. 46 W.	39.17648001, -86.2657938
North Gate—1801 State Hwy. 46 E.	39.19313325, -86.21656259
Horse Camp—4800 State Hwy. 135 S.	39.12899036, -86.19548562

Created from the meltwater of ancient glaciers, the narrow ridges and deep gullies of Indiana's largest park have become a fall color hot spot. Encompassing 15,815 acres of heavily wooden terrain and scenic vistas, Brown County State Park reigns in majestic beauty and hushed, inviting woodlands. With a large collection of lookout vistas that face in almost every direction, visitors come from all over the country to experience the glow of autumn color. With the tiny town of Nashville, Indiana, only a few miles away, both major tourism to the town and one of Indiana's largest tracts of land bring over a million visitors to the area every year. One of the most popular events at the park continues to be the spring Morel Mushroom Festival, where visitors can learn about many edible fungi through interpretive programs as well as purchase a bag of morel mushrooms through the Friends of Brown County State Park.

The project of creating Brown County State Park began when a young Brown County man named Lee Bright became concerned about the destruction of the property's forests. Wanting to find a way to preserve the area for future generations and help his neighbors sell their land,

The picturesque lookouts at Brown County State Park have made the area nationally known for its autumn colors.

Bright attempted several times to meet with Richard Lieber and present his idea for a state park. Unable to get past Lieber's secretary, Bright discussed his idea with a game warden, Fred Ahlers. Knowing that the state had the funds to purchase land for use as game reserves, Ahlers introduced Bright to George Mannfield. As the state's first superintendent of Fisheries and Game, Mannfield provided the connection Bright needed to finally speak with Lieber. Bright was appointed an agent of the state in 1924 to acquire the land for a game reserve and was able to help his neighbors pull themselves from financial troubles, buying the first 50 acres for $10.17 per acre—a small fortune at the time. While most of the land

The lakes at Brown County State Park help create a gorgeous, natural setting.

acquired had been abandoned or sold at tax sales, 18 owner-occupied parcels were purchased—including the village of Kelp, which had a small school and a church that no longer exist. Formally securing 7,600 acres, the Brown County Game Reserve opened later that same year.

Game birds, such as pheasants and quail, began to be raised on the property through game farms that followed a popular trend of raising wildlife for release to areas where animals had been displaced due to agriculture. A wildlife exhibit on game preserve property housed coyote, black bear, fox, and many other animals, while buffalo, deer, and elk were penned in the area that would become Buffalo Ridge Campground. The animal exhibits were eventually phased out in 1975.

While the discussion of creating a state park began in 1928, it wasn't until the following year that Brown County's commissioner relinquished 1,129 acres that bordered the game reserve to be used for the state park's development. Named for General Jacob Brown, a veteran of the War of 1812 and commanding general of the US Army, the park was officially dedicated in 1929. By 1940, additional land from the game reserve was added totaling 13,000 acres. As time passed the park's landholdings increased, making it the largest state park in the state by thousands of acres.

The Civilian Conservation Corps (CCC) began working in the park in 1934, using local lumber and sandstone to construct the amphitheater, picnic shelters, saddle barn, and lookout towers. Two lookout towers exist in the north and west sections of the park. Built of sandstone and log cabin-style construction, the original north lookout tower, built by the CCC, was primarily made of logs alone and had to be rebuilt in 1988 to resemble the sandstone-log western tower after insect damage made it unsafe for the public to use.

Erosion control was aided by planting black locust, black walnut, pine, and spruce trees throughout the park. The pine forest that still stands today, along the edge of Strahl Lake, grew from the seedlings originally planted by the CCC. Between 1934 and 1935, Lake Ogle was created providing a new water supply for the park. While CCC workers were first housed in the village of Kelp, they were later moved to a collection of barracks until the program ended in 1945.

After Brown County State Park had been officially dedicated, the Abe Martin Lodge, meant as a memorial to Indiana humorist Frank McKinney "Kin" Hubbard, was dedicated in 1932. As the creator of the famous 1900s cartoon *Abe Martin of Brown County*, Hubbard had his work

The Abe Martin Lodge has been a historic fixture to Brown County State Park for generations.

published in US newspapers from 1904 until his death in 1930. While he worked and lived in Indianapolis, he was known to frequent the area using the surrounding woods as a muse. The park's Abe Martin Lodge is named to honor Hubbard's fictional woodsman character used to convey Hubbard's humor and comical quips. Born in 1868 in Bellefontaine, Ohio, Hubbard was a self-taught artist, learning the trade of printing in his father's print shop while working in a post office. During the years before the creation of Abe Martin, Hubbard led a colorful life doing all sorts of creative passions, including writing, producing, and acting in minstrel shows. While he worked as a sketch artist for several newspapers in Ohio, he returned to working for the *Indianapolis News* in 1901—where he stayed for the remainder of his career. Starting as short comics, Hubbard's sketches soon accompanied longer comedic essays, which he named "Short Furrows." By 1910, his popular cartoon series was syndicated in over 200 newspapers. When Kin Hubbard passed away in 1930, he had created over 16,000 sayings, 1,000 "Short Furrows," and 8,000 drawings. His wit and philosophy on life was soon missed by millions, including the famed humorist and cowboy Will Rogers, who was quoted as saying, "Kin Hubbard was at the top for real downright humor. He'd forgotten more humor than the rest of 'em probably ever will know."

When Brown County State Park was first established in 1929, the space where Abe Martin Lodge now sits served only as a commissary, a place for guests to buy their groceries. During the lodge's first stages of development, a shower facility was available and rustic cabins provided the first housing at Brown County State Park. As time passed, the commissary was converted into a dining room and the cabins were remodeled. By the 1960s sleeping rooms were added to the lodge's dining facilities, and the Abe Martin Lodge became the fine establishment we know today. More sleeping rooms, a conference room, and 20 additional cabins were added in the 1980s, and in 2008 the lodge received its most extensive overhaul with the addition of a wonderful aquatic center. Built from hand-hewed native stone and oak timber cut in the park, the Abe Martin Lodge currently offers hotel-style rooms, partly in the main lodge and the annex building, and it has a long list of cabins available to rent year-round. All of the cabins are named after principle comic characters created by Kin Hubbard. The cabins are advertised as "Abe Martin Family Cabins on Skunk Ridge."

Keeping with traditional interpretive demonstration, the park offers a nature center with a rich exhibition of the park's history and animal life. Over a dozen displays show preserved gray fox, chipmunks, ruffed grouse, owls, and many birds in realistic settings. Several live animal habitats house native snakes, including a live timber rattlesnake—occasionally sighted throughout the property.

The park offers a large conglomerate of camping, with over 400 camping sites within the Buffalo Ridge, Raccoon Ridge, and Taylor Ridge Campgrounds. There are electric and nonelectric sites, and in the warmer months, they fill up fast. There are more sites without electric, making it worth spending a little more for a site with full electric in order to put some distance between other campers. A country store is open during the warm season. Group camping is offered in the Rally Campground.

The Henry Wolf Bridge, which visitors travel across while entering through the north entrance of the park, is the oldest covered bridge in Indiana. Constructed in 1838, the bridge was moved from Putnam County to its current location in 1932. Twenty-eight miles of International Mountain Bicycling Association paths exist within park boundaries, as well as 70 miles of horse paths and a horsemen's campground.

The architecture of Brown County State Park was designed to easily blend into the park's natural beauty.

OGLE HOLLOW NATURE PRESERVE

Located in the central section of the park, this 41-acre tract is a small island of rare and protected species. Cool moist conditions on the north-facing slope make the preserve particularly rich and abundant with life. The rare yellowwood tree is an outstanding feature of this preserve, and Ogle Hollow remains one of the few places in Indiana where these trees are found. In addition to the yellowwood, chestnut oak and black oak are found on the upper slope, while red and white oaks grow throughout the lower elevations. The understory has beautiful flowering dogwood and redbud, mixed with pawpaw, spicebush, ironwood, and musclewood. Wildflowers also add their color during the growing season, and Christmas ferns, maidenhair ferns, and glade ferns are widely distributed on the rocky slopes.

HORSEMEN'S CAMP

The horsemen's campground at Brown County State Park has 118 modern campsites with electrical hookup and modern restrooms/showers, as well as 64 primitive campsites with pit toilets without showers or modern restrooms.

Old fences add to the natural
aesthetics that make Brown
County State Park such a
beautiful place.

Some of the best hiking one can experience in Indiana is in Brown County State Park. More than 21 miles of easy-to-rugged hiking trails meander through Brown County State Park and are for hiking only. From tall, vista lookouts to low bottomland, the park has every type of hiking experience one can imagine. The autumn brings on a change in the color of the area's leaves that has become nationally known as one of the most beautiful places to experience the change of the season. Hiking trails include short paths around the lodge to long and rugged adventures through one of Indiana's oldest parks.

TRAIL 1—LODGE TRAIL
(0.9 miles) Moderate—The Lodge Trail starts behind the Abe Martin Lodge near the Uncle Niles Turner Cabin. The trail leads through a wooded path of oak, hickory, sassafras, beech, and maple trees before looping back to the first section of the trail. Many old stone structures from the park's rich past can be seen just a short distance away.

TRAIL 2—CCC TRAIL
(2 miles) Moderate—This trail starts behind the Abe Martin Lodge near the Lafe Bud, Tawney Apple, and the Doc Mopps Cabins. The trail passes behind the family cabins to cross the lodge road, passing the north lookout tower at 1.19 miles. The path passes the Lower Shelter House before climbing a set of stairs to return behind the lodge.

TRAIL 3—SADDLE BARN LOOP
(1.25 miles) Moderate—The trail begins behind the Abe Martin Lodge and passes by the CCC-built amphitheater and saddle barn. At 0.21 miles there is a grass field crossing, heading toward the fence and road. Crossing the bridge, the trail turns right and the pathway enters the woods again at 0.28 miles. The trail follows the road for 2,349 feet before emerging to cross a 200-foot field before entering the woods again. The trail crosses over the horse trail used by the saddle barn and joins Trail 2 to return to the rear of the Abe Martin Lodge.

TRAIL 4—RALLY CAMPGROUND TRAIL
(1.52 miles) Moderate—The trail begins at the edge of the Ogle Ridge/ Rally Campground parking area. The path leads through upland terrain,

to a deep ravine at the headwaters of Ogle Lake. The trail then connects with Trail 7 at 0.74 miles and follows the path for roughly 820 feet before branching off toward the nature preserve, ending at the junction of Trail 5.

TRAIL 5—OGLE HALLOW NATURE PRESERVE TRAIL
(0.66 miles) Rugged—Although this is one of the park's shortest trails, an elevation change of 259 feet makes it particularly rugged. The trail runs directly through the 41-acre Ogle Hallow Nature Preserve, established to protect the park's rarest yellowwood trees. An endangered species, the yellowwood tree has a limited range throughout the United States, and the state's only naturally occurring yellowwoods are located in Brown County State Park. Named for the bright yellow heartwood, the tree was once used in making dyes, gunstocks, and furniture.

TRAIL 6—STRAHL LAKE TRAIL
(0.8 miles) Easy/Rugged—The trail is accessed from the Strahl Lake parking area and after 49 steps the trail circles Strahl Lake, passing tall pines and spruce planted by the CCC in the 1930s. Areas of the trail that often succumb to flooding have boardwalks installed for easy crossing of the lake's shoreline. A 0.5 connecting trail near the back end of the lake leads uphill to the Nature Center. Before a lake existed on the property, a portion of the land was owned by a farmer named Jimmy Strahl. Having only a marginally productive farm, he sold his land to the state and in return the state paid him handsomely and named the lake in his honor. The dam at Strahl Lake was constructed in 1928.

TRAIL 7—OGLE LAKE TRAIL
(1.5 miles) Moderate—This trail begins on the stone steps at the edge of the parking area of Ogle Lake and loops around the lake through a root-covered dirt trail and over a large collection of wooden planked walkways. The north section of the trail is dry and winds along the lower edges of the lake, leading lower into the park's eastern wetlands. The southern edge of the trail climbs up and down wooden steps along the steep hillside edge of Ogle Lake, crossing over the dam and leading back to the parking area.

TRAIL 8—HOOSIER HIKERS COUNCIL TRAIL

(3.5 miles) Moderate—This trail begins at the far side of the picnic area of Ogle Lake and leads north into a divided set of loop trails. The trail passes by the location of Hesitation Point, and at 2.19 miles a spur trail to the west lookout tower connects back to Trail 8.

TRAIL 9—TAYLOR RIDGE TRAIL

(3.0/2.5 miles) Rugged—The trail begins and ends at the Taylor Ridge Campground near Campsite 324, with an additional portion leading to Ogle Lake. At one time, the trail only included a connection trail from the campground leading to a looping section, giving the trail a three-mile distance. In 2004, the Hoosier Hikers Council added a wonderful 2.5-mile trail, connecting the previous loop north to Ogle Lake.

TRAIL 10—FIRE TOWER TRAIL

(2.2 miles) Rugged—This area boasts the county's top elevation, reaching 1,058 feet above sea level, and was once the location of wheat fields and peach orchards. Beginning and ending on Weedpatch Hill near a fire tower built in 1927, the trail also features another piece of CCC history—an old stone building with a fireplace known as the Peachtree Shelter ("Treasures in Your Own Backyard," Marty Benson, 2016).

FRIENDS OF BROWN COUNTY STATE PARK
EASY ACCESS TRAIL

(978 feet) Easy—Dedicated June 3, 2000, the trail is a short paved path around the back side of the park's visitors' center. The path is a brief loop with an additional intersecting trail. In this centrally located path sits the park's original west gatehouse. Built in 1933, it was moved and restored in 2006 by Friends of Brown County State Park. Completely wheelchair accessible, the trail travels across several wooden decks with wooden benches constructed along the edge of the wildflower-rich forest.

DISCOVERY TRAIL

(0.5 miles) Moderate—This is a self-guided nature trail with plenty of things to see along the way. A brochure is available at the trailhead at the south end of the nature center parking lot.

9

Mounds State Park

Established 1930—290 acres

4306 Mounds Road

Anderson, IN 46017

(765) 642-6627

40.100386, -85.620722

With 10 earthworks built by indigenous people, Mounds State Park is one of Indiana's most unique historical treasures. Key landscape features to see are Great Mound, Fiddle Back Mound, Circle Mound, and several other unnamed earthwork formations. Constructed by Native people who lived in the region more than 2,000 years ago, the Great Mound complex is one of the largest and most well-preserved mound features in the area based on the excavation of similar mound features. The sizes and shapes of the ancient earthworks vary a bit from circles, rectangles, and odd-shaped knolls. Each mound is similar, however, in construction, built with an outer embankment that surrounds a ditch. In the center of the Great Mound is a flat, central platform believed to be used by a shaman or priest to perform his or her ceremony. Each mound contains a break in its outer embankment serving as a gateway for a person to enter into the mound. The mounds were constructed by removing the soil from the interior, creating ditches, then moving the soil to the outside to form the higher outer embankment forming the mounds.

Once thought to be burial mounds, the earthen structures are now believed to have been used for celestial and astrological religious ceremonies. Their main purpose was some sort of ritual connected with the

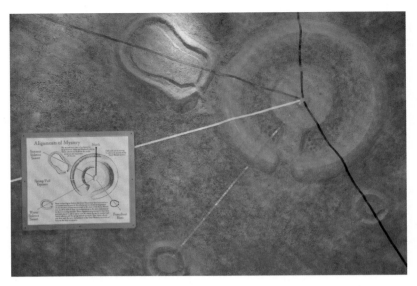

A large map shows the layout of the ancient mounds and how they align with celestial points.

sun, as the outer individual mounds are approximately placed to allow one to view the sunsets in accordance with the summer and winter solstices. Standing in the center of the Great Mound, its outer walls serve quite well as an artificial horizon for seasonal religious ceremonies using the sun as a guide. The Great Mound measured 300 feet across and 1,200 feet around. Through radiocarbon dating, the mound construction has been determined to be from sometime around 160 to 120 BC. Although we may never fully know the truth of the mound's particular use, a definite alignment exists with the sky and the main earthworks outside of the Great Mound—Fiddle Back Mound, Earthwork B, and another unnamed earthen structure. Fiddle Back Mound is the most unique of the three, built in the pattern of a figure eight or the shape of a fiddle. Out of hundreds of earthworks that exist in Indiana and Ohio, only five have a similar shape to Fiddle Back Mound. In connection with the Great Mound, Fiddle Back Mound is in the pathway of the summer solstice sunset if viewed from the Great Mound center platform. Earthwork B is the smallest enclosure in the park and measures only 85 feet across. It is unique in that it has two gateway openings, with the gateway on the eastside added later after the mound's construction. From the center platform of the Great Mound, Earthwork B aligns with the Fomalhaut star, the brightest star in the Piscis Austrinus constellation and one of

THE COMPLETE GUIDE TO INDIANA STATE PARKS

Stars shine brightly, high
above the ancient mounds
at Mounds State Park.

the brightest stars in the sky. The unnamed earthwork located southwest of the Great Mound is similar in design to Earthwork B but with only one gateway. This mound structure aligns with the winter solstice sunset. Another mound structure still exists much farther away than the other structures from the Great Mound, in the northern section of the park. Known as the Circle Mound, it is actually rectangular in shape and was built after the Great Mound. Its gateway opens to the east and is directly aligned with the sunrise on the spring and autumn equinox.

The Adena culture is believed to be responsible for the mounds' construction. Evidence shows that another culture either evolved from the Adena or simply arrived after they were gone. These Hopewell people also made an impact on the mounds approximately 170 years after the creation of the Great Mound, using the site for ceremonial burials. Between 1968 and 1969, Indiana University archaeologists first discovered a small burial plot on top of the Great Mound connected to the Hopewell culture. The excavation uncovered a log tomb with pieces of mica, deer leg-bones tools, and human remains.

THE BRONNENBERGS

Born in Germany in 1775, Frederick Brandenburg apprenticed as a tanner as a young boy. His mother, wanting him to avoid being recruited by the military, sent him to the United States, where he changed his name from Brandenburg to Bronnenberg. Migrating west to Pennsylvania to establish a tanning business, he met his wife Barbara Eastor and started a family in 1806. Continuing to move west, the family lived in Virginia and Ohio, heading west toward Illinois in 1819, where Frederick, his wife, and eight children made it only as far as what is now Madison County, Indiana. Several stories explain why the family stopped where they did, including a tale of a broken-down oxen and wagon, as well as the death of their younger daughter due to illness. Now settled in Indiana, Frederick purchased the property of what would become Mounds State Park, taking over an abandoned fur trapper's log cabin.

Having 12 children, 9 of whom survived, the property remained in the hands of the family with the sixth-born child, Frederick Jr., building the famed Bronnenberg House in 1850—a beautiful brick, two-story, Federal-style, ell-shaped home. Built using tulip and oak lumber, as well as other native materials, the house originally consisted of two main rooms on the first floor and two on the second with an additional room in the back called an ell. Local limestone was used for the foundation and

Built around 1840, the Bronnenburg House is recognized by the National Register of Historic Places for its architectural and cultural significance.

sandstone was used for the window sills, with the bricks made from local clay. Cedar trees provided the material for the original wooden roof shingles. Frederick Jr.'s son Ransom later added to the house by enclosing the back porch and adding a second floor to the porch and the ell. This additional construction expanded the house for Ransom's six children and is the way the house can be seen today. While the house remains as the only surviving structure from the Bronnenberg homestead, the farm once included a springhouse, outdoor kitchen, smokehouse, corncrib barn, and many other structures.

Frederick Sr. ran a successful tannery, sawmill, and gristmill while his son Frederick Jr. farmed the family's large property. Being a successful lineage of successful business operators, these operations made the Bronnenbergs wealthy and prominent in the local area. When Frederick Jr. died in 1901, his son Ransom was left in charge of the property. In 1897, Ransom began leasing out 40 acres of the property to the Union Traction Company with an option to buy in five years. This leased land was located in the southern corner of Mounds State Park.

THE UNION TRACTION COMPANY AND
MOUNDS AMUSEMENT PARK

The Union Traction Company's train system, known as the Interurban, once traveled through the western area of the Great Mound complex. For five cents, passengers would travel roundtrip from the nearby town of Anderson to visit the mounds and later the Mounds Amusement Park. One of the first electric trains, the Interurban made it possible for people to commute from small towns to larger cities and enjoy attractions that were a much farther distance away. One of the premier attractions in the area at the time, Mounds Amusement Park operated from 1897 until 1929. The forest that exists today was once cleared to make room for the famed rollercoaster called "Leap the Dips," a merry-go-round, penny arcade, shooting gallery, a horseshoe field, skating rink, and many other park attractions. The park included a restaurant and a miniature steam train that circled the Great Mound. The park also had a two-story pavilion located on the bluff between Great Mound and the White River— with a restaurant and large dining room on the first floor and a dance hall on the second that hosted events on Friday and Saturday nights. As with many amusement parks of the era, the Great Depression took its toll on Mounds Amusement Park, and it was inevitably closed. The Union Traction Company sold the property to the Madison County Historical Society, who later donated it to the state of Indiana. Financial problems by the Union Traction Company were also unbearable during the Depression era, and with the dawn of the automobile, the company was forced to close the Interurban after a need for mass transit disappeared. The last run of the Interurban was on November 13, 1941. Remnants of the old Interurban Waiting Station and of Mounds Amusement Park still exist, with concrete footers and foundations scattered through the now reclaimed forest.

It is because Frederick Bronnenberg Jr. recognized the importance of preserving the mounds that they continue to exist today. Fighting to protect them from looters and farm plow destruction, he passed on his passion for preserving the ancient structures to his children, who continued to protect them until the land was turned over to the state. Richard Lieber first inspected the property in 1921 and found it to be worthy of further preservation as an Indiana State Park. With 258 acres already owned by the state of Indiana thanks to the Madison County Historical Society, the land became Indiana's ninth state park in 1930.

Flowing along the western border of Mounds State Park, the White River is a popular place for boating.

CAVES

Several caves once existed on park property. These include a five-room cave discovered by Clyde Denny, "John Kane's Tunnel," an additional cave that once appeared on an early postcard beneath Mounds K and I, another cave with circular rooms described by E. T. Cox, a cave in which Frances Norton was lost, and a cave that was covered over by debris from the amusement park.

POINTS OF INTEREST

A large memorial rock is placed outside of the nature center in memory of Michael Patterson, a dedicated employee of Mounds State Park for 31 years. The memorial reads, "His efforts are visible in all you see here."

The nature center offers a wildlife viewing room, animal displays, interactive games, and naturalist-led hikes and interpretive programs. A canoe constructed using 2,000-year-old Adena methods sits outside of the nature center and was built by park volunteers. A pavilion near the park entrance was built by the National Youth Administration in the late 1930s and can accommodate 150 people for private events.

The nearby White River offers the opportunity for fishing, and the park contains six miles of hiking trails. Seventy-five Class A electric camping sites exist with partly shaded, asphalt pads as well as a youth tent area and dump stations. The swimming pool remains a popular attraction and is able to accommodate 500 people.

TRAIL 1
(1 mile) Easy—The main hiking trail passes most of the mounds complex features, such as Great Mound, Fiddle Back Mound, and Earthwork B. The path is made up of several loops that wind through the complex surrounded by a very diverse collection of Indiana's 20 most common trees. Well shaded, the trail is great for easy strolling through the forest.

TRAIL 2
(0.5 miles) Rugged—Beginning at the pavilion, the trail descends over a boardwalk, heading west down a set of steps connecting with Trail 5 near the White River and also heading south over a boardwalk connecting with Trail 1 near the east side of the mounds complex.

TRAIL 3
(0.9 miles) Moderate—The path is a maze of four crisscrossing loops that connect Trail 5 to several exiting points and parking areas. Skirting the pavilion in its southernmost section, the trail also provides access to the Friends Shelter and Woodland Shelter. While not a difficult trail, the dirt path does clamber over the rocky terrain uphill from the White River.

TRAIL 4
(0.7 miles) Rugged—The path connects the campground to the swimming pool by way of a centrally located, north-to-south secondary trail with a long-stretching boardwalk. The main trail, leading from the park road and Trail 5 near the White River, runs from west to east, with a loop in the middle connecting back with Trail 5 in the easternmost section of the park.

TRAIL 5

(2.5 miles) Moderate—Once an old state park bridle path, remnants of the old Waiting Station from the Interurban rail line can still be seen as a section of this trail was once the old electric train's railbed. A wide path covered in gravel, the trail is one of the most used in the park, looping around the entire property while providing easy access to all of the park's main features and trails—beginning and ending at the park's gatehouse entrance and the park's visitors' center. In the western section of the park, the White River runs parallel with Trail 5, as water seeps from the hillside and flows underneath the trail. The path crosses over several culverts that divert the hillside creek water into the White River as the trail sits just a few feet from the river's shoreline.

TRAIL 6

(0.4 miles) Moderate—The path is a Y-shaped trail that connects the youth tent area and the nearby public campground to Trail 5. The trail is great for a short hike from the campground or to make rounds throughout the entire camping area, including the camp store and the Campground Control Station. A secondary trail at the Trail 5 intersection leads west to the canoe launch area—a wide-open, heavily used gravel bar with a parking area.

10

Lincoln State Park

Established 1932—1,747 acres

15476 North County Rd 300 East

Lincoln City, IN 47552

(812) 937-4710

38.104167, -86.996389

Established in 1932, Lincoln State Park is a memorial to Abraham Lincoln's mother, Nancy Hanks. Currently 2,026 acres, Lincoln State Park was established to protect land used by the Lincoln family during their stay in Indiana between 1816 and 1830. When purchased, the site included the Nancy Hanks Lincoln grave and the Lincoln cabin site. Both sites were transferred to the National Park Service in 1962 to become the Lincoln Boyhood National Memorial.

Remnants of the community that developed in the area following Indiana's statehood in 1816 are the key features—including the church where Lincoln served as the sexton, the site where an old mill once sat, and the land that once held the foundation of a no longer existing general store, post office, and schoolhouse. Known as the Little Pigeon Creek Settlement, the camp has a long history of Lincoln family life and the cemetery holds many residents from the area, including the Romines, the Gentrys, the Barkers, the Oskins, the Lamars, and Abraham Lincoln's sister, Sarah Lincoln Grigsby.

Sarah was Lincoln's only sister, and it was said that they were so close that when Lincoln's mother died, she became almost like his mother.

A view from the fire tower at Lincoln State Park.

Sarah Lincoln died in childbirth on January 20, 1828, as did her child. On the night of her passing, young Abraham was at the house of Rueben Grigsby Sr. doing carpentry work in the smokehouse, when Sarah's husband Aaron came running up the road to spread the distressing news. As the story goes, young Lincoln sat in the doorway of the smokehouse and sobbed, raining tears through his fingers. Sarah's child was buried in her arms, and her husband Aaron lays next to her. Sarah's grave was originally marked with a slab of sandstone until it was replaced with a memorial headstone in 1916.

A lakeside view of Lake Lincoln.

During the 1930s the Civilian Conservation Corps (CCC) played an active role in building many of the park's facilities. Since the area was primarily used for farming prior to the establishment of the park, CCC Company 1543 planted 1,750 acres, as well as built trails and campgrounds. The dam that created Lake Lincoln proved to be their largest project, requiring 27,000 cubic yards of earth, providing a reliable water supply for the park. The lakeside shelter and the boat rental building (formerly a ranger cabin) were also built by the CCC, with the ranger cabin now the oldest remaining CCC ranger cabin in Indiana. By October of their first year the camp was awarded the "Most Outstanding of the 5th Area," an area that included 116 camps. The CCC finished their work at Lincoln State Park in 1934 and were transferred to Turkey Run State Park, leaving a legacy behind them. Before the CCC camp was decommissioned in 1941, there were 200 men living at the camp, which consisted of four barracks, a mess hall, administration building, recreation hall, garages, and a bathhouse. Additional work included the planting of the pine plantations, applying erosion controls, and establishing the 115-acre Nancy Hanks Memorial. Remains of the camp are found near the park entrance along the beginning northern section of the James Gentry Trail.

SARAH LINCOLN WOODS NATURE PRESERVE

Located in the southernmost portion of the park, the preserve was identified by the Division of Nature Preserves as best representing presettlement conditions—while also protecting an uncommon Indiana plant community called the oak barrens. Dedicated in 1988 as an official state nature preserve, the 110-acre area of woodland memorializes Lincoln's sister. Very similar kinds of trees and vegetation are present today as existed in Lincoln's time, including oak and hickory, with ash dominating the forest. Although the forest has since been heavily logged, it has matured back to a reasonably healthy forest since being preserved. Most of the landscape continues to be a dry to semi-dry forest with species that thrive in drier conditions, such as black oaks, scarlet oaks, and sugar maples. While forests of this type were once very plentiful in Lincoln's era, they have become increasingly uncommon today. Rare herbs grow in remote locations of the preserve, including butterfly pea known to grown in only five other sites in the state. An attractive plant with large, purple flowers that bloom in July, the plant gets its name from the pea-pod-like fruit that it produces in late summer and fall.

ABRAHAM LINCOLN BICENTENNIAL PLAZA

An unmistakable feature witnessed while driving through the park is the Abraham Lincoln Bicentennial Plaza, dedicated January 12, 2009. A 58-foot diameter stone circular plaza resides in a clearing on the left after entering the park's main gate. The reasoning behind the memorial was not only to give remembrance to the nation's 16th president but also to provide an educational and inspirational experience. The memorial is designed to show Lincoln's height through each passing year, with

The Abraham Lincoln Bicentennial Plaza was constructed in 2009 to honor the two-hundredth birthday of President Abraham Lincoln and his years as a boy in Indiana.

large limestone pillars rising in height until reaching six feet four inches, Lincoln's height when he reached the age of 21 and left Indiana. The limestone structure was constructed using stone from the Empire Quarry in Oolitic, Indiana, which also supplied the stone for the Empire State Building. With the largest stone weighing 3,400 pounds, there are 94 pieces of limestone throughout the memorial. The central theme of the plaza comes from the poem by William Wordsworth, entitled "My Heart Leaps Up," written in 1802, and the words "The child is father of the man" line the limestone crown of the memorial. A bronze bust weighing 400 pounds, cast at the Shidoni Foundry near Santa Fe, New Mexico, rests directly next to two of Lincoln's most noted speeches—the Gettysburg Address and the closing words of Lincoln's second inaugural address. Quotes from Lincoln and the people who knew him best surround the memorial and revel in Lincoln's inspiration to others as an incredibly honest and extraordinary individual.

LINCOLN STATE PARK AMPHITHEATER

As one of the largest roofed amphitheaters in the nation, Lincoln Amphitheatre is a grand 1,500-seat outdoor venue that often books

The Lincoln Amphitheatre.

internationally known acts, as well as producing a story about Abraham Lincoln's life and times. Lincoln State Park is truly unique in having a full-performance venue for visitors to enjoy.

The park also offers a nature center with interpretive hikes, a swimming beach, canoe rental, and a boat launch ramp for boating and fishing. The campground offers 150 sites with electric, 88 nonelectric, primitive sites at Gobblers Run Campground, group camping and cottages at Pine Hill, and family cabins at Blue Heron. The trails at Lincoln State Park carry a great deal of history, as some were constructed on roads and pathways used by Lincoln himself.

TRAIL 1—LAKE TRAIL
(1.5 miles) Easy—Marked as Trail 1, the east section of the path begins at Lake Lincoln's boat rental building, once used as the old CCC ranger cabin. The trail follows the east shore of Lake Lincoln before reaching a short, loop trail leading to a fire tower built by the CCC in 1935. With the fire tower resting on a high bluff, the path leading up to it swiftly gains in elevation, climbing a steep hill. Due to the steep terrain, the path

is commonly washed out with loose mud and rock, yet the trail is still stable and well maintained. Since only just over a dozen fire towers still stand in Indiana, the rare occasion to visit one in such a beautiful, natural setting should not be missed. The tower offers a panoramic view of the park, best viewed in the autumn months, only after climbing its 106 steps to a tight booth. Once back on the Lake Trail, wood-planked and gravel walkways continue along the south shore passing Trail 3 (Sarah Lincoln Grigsby Trail) before passing the nature center. A smooth path along the lush shoreline moves north from the nature center along the west bank of Lake Lincoln, past another opportunity to access Trail 3, and leads along the dam that holds the lake, heading back to the beach area where the trail begins.

TRAIL 2—JOHN CARTER TRAIL

(2.1 miles) Moderate—Named after a neighbor of the Lincoln family, the trail begins east of the gatehouse, near the park office, and travels through the northeast section of the park. The trail is highlighted by the fact that it is the farthest trail from all park facilities and offers hikers the ability to add other trails, creating the most rugged hike in the park. A spur trail midway leads west toward the Buckhorn Youth Tent Area while the southern end of the trail connects with Trail 1 (Lake Trail).

TRAIL 3—SARAH LINCOLN GRIGSBY TRAIL

(1.7 miles) Moderate—Two access points exist for this trail—the southern section of Trail 1 (Lake Trail) and near the dam of Lake Lincoln just north of the nature center. Noted as the park's most unspoiled and uncommon area, the upland forest and steep ravines lead the trail directly through a large portion of the Sarah Lincoln Woods Nature Preserve.

TRAIL 4—JAMES GENTRY TRAIL

(3.7 miles) Moderate—A historical marker at the most western end of the trail designates the location of the Grigsby store and is known as the last place the Lincoln family stayed the night before leaving Indiana. The site of the former CCC camp can be seen from the eastern section of the loop near the park office. Midway through, the trail allows access to Weber Lake and the park's wetlands, a point of interest of a once dead lake brought back to pristine conditions through intense reclamation. Although not particularly difficult, the trail is noted as the park's longest trail and travels over active railroads and busy State Road 162. The

Gentry Homesite can also be accessed by driving to a very small parking area, 1.3 miles west of the park. From the parking area, the site is close to one-quarter mile along a smooth, heavily forested path. The site itself is a large stone with a metal plaque, honoring the location.

TRAIL 5—MR. LINCOLN'S NEIGHBORHOOD WALK

(1.7 miles) Moderate—The trail highlights the park's Lincoln-era sites, such as Noah Gorden's Mill and Homesite, the Little Pigeon Primitive Baptist Church, and the cemetery where the grave of Sarah Lincoln Grigsby rests. A farmer and miller, Noah Gorden lived at the site between 1816 and 1829 in a log home with his family of six. Before moving away to Missouri, Noah sold the property to John Romine, who continued to operate the mill for several more years. The mill, built in 1818, was a horse-operated corn-grinding mill and is the famous location where Abraham Lincoln was kicked by a horse and almost fatally injured at the age of 11. The Little Pigeon Primitive Baptist Church was originally built in 1821, with Lincoln's father Thomas responsible for building the walnut pulpit, window castings, and cabinetwork. The church is also where Lincoln served as a sexton, where his duties included taking care of the property, ringing the church bell for services, and digging the graves of the cemetery. Initially constructed out of hewed logs, the building was replaced by another building around the end of the 1870s. A third building—the one present today—was built in 1948, 90 feet from the church's original location.

The trail begins and ends near the parking area of the Little Pigeon Church and follows a gravel path most of the way toward the west and south along what was once known as Gentry Store–Troy Road. The old roadway is a wide path traveling through shallow creeks. Once southward for a stretch, a long wooden platform meanders up to a slightly higher elevation and out of the creek beds. While a service road exists nearby, the actual trail leads directly through the Gorden Homesite and past the well. From here the trail narrows and leads through lush, shaded forests of large pines and thin deciduous trees, traveling across the shallow creeks by way of several sturdy, wooden bridges. The trail crosses over a larger creek—Buckhorn Creek—several times, and the water drains into the 58-acre Lake Lincoln.

TRAIL 6—WEBER LAKE TRAIL

(1.8 miles) Easy—The Weber Lake Trail is named for a once sterile area destroyed by the operations of an old surface mine that operated between 1930 and 1958. Before the reclamation process began, the lake was completely devoid of life. In February 1965, the state acquired 115 acres of land and Weber Lake to add to Lincoln State Park, where it sat until proper funding and support could begin a reclamation process in 2001. Due to high acidity in the lake, the water needed to be treated with alkaline chemicals to begin raising the pH of the water and a wetland was constructed to filter incoming water into the lake. Funding for the restoration of Weber Lake came from the Abandoned Mine Lands program, administered by the Indiana Department of Natural Resources Division of Reclamation. Today the lake is alive and thriving with fish and aquatic species that would normally be vulnerable to poor water conditions. Evidence of mining remains, as piles of coal and other materials, as well as an old weigh scale, line the area of Trail 4 (James Gentry Trail). The north and west sections of the Weber Lake Trail also connect and give access to Trail 4 (James Gentry Trail). The Weber Lake Trail (Trail 6) is the primary route to loop around the lake, starting at a parking area near the Spring Shelter, running parallel with a long stretch of railroad tracks.

11

Tippecanoe River State Park

Established 1943—2,785 acres

4200 N. US 35

Winamac, IN 46996

(574) 946-3213

41.12232, -86.58297

Prior to settlement, the Tippecanoe River was a major route for the fur trade between the French and the Potawatomi people. The area was so popular that by the 1830s settlers had taken over the land completely— the Potawatomi had been moved to a Kansas reservation—and began farming larger areas and grazing livestock. The area remained farmland and changed very little until the Great Depression.

Between 1934 and 1942, the US Department of the Interior acquired close to 7,353 acres of land in an area bordering the Tippecanoe River. Most of the infrastructure of the park we see today was originally etched out by the Works Progress Administration (WPA) developing roads and facility buildings. Thanks to the work of many people hired with the WPA, the recreational facility was essentially complete when it changed hands from the federal government to Indiana's Department of Conservation. On March 18, 1943, the property officially became Indiana's eleventh state park. On January 1, 1959, 4,592 acres were trans- ferred to the Department of Natural Resources (DNR) Division of Fish and Wildlife and named the Winamac Fish and Wildlife Area. The re- maining 2,761 acres were kept under the ownership of the state park. In

Trees warmed by an early morning sunrise cast reflections in shallow pools of the Tippecanoe River.

1985, major renovations were done to the park's cross-country ski rental and warming hut, converting it into a nature center.

The land within the borders of Tippecanoe River State Park holds many treasures, including a preserved grove of old-growth pine trees and more than two miles of undisturbed wetland and shoreline. A 20-acre waterfowl refuge was added to the park in the 1970s and continues to be a special place for visitors interested in birding.

THE TIPPECANOE RIVER

The river is regarded as one of the most biologically diverse rivers in the country. Originally the river was named Kith-tip-pe-ca-nunk, meaning "place of the buffalo fish" in the Shawnee language. The Tippecanoe River follows a 225-mile route from Lake Tippecanoe, traveling south to the Wabash River, and with countless twists and turns, it passes through 14 counties. One of the reasons the river continues to remain clean and healthy is because of its enormous mussel population. Mussels filter the water, keeping it clean for themselves as well as other plants and animals, and at Tippecanoe River State Park mussels are highly praised through education programs and displays. The largest population of clubshell mussel lives in the Tippecanoe River. Most mussels contained in the river are federally endangered species, and few Midwestern rivers contain as many endangered species as the Tippecanoe River.

BANK STABILIZATION

The Tippecanoe River is always changing its course, and the natural river movement has proved to be a challenge for the life of the park. In less than 20 years, a bend in the river had etched away the bank, moving 50 feet into the park while destroying the park's picnic area. In 2002, a bank stabilization project was implemented, addressing the erosion control issues by installing a permanent bank structure of glacial stone. This bank now houses two wooden fishing piers and a canoe launch near the River Shelter and nature center.

RIVER OTTER RELEASE

At one time, river otters were extremely rare in Indiana. Due to over-hunting and loss of habitat, Indiana's river otter nearly went extinct by the 1940s. Until as recently as 1995, river otters were virtually nonexistent in the park area until Indiana's DNR started to bring the animals back. On a cold January 29, 1996, otters returned to Tippecanoe River State Park as part of the DNR release program.

SAND HILL NATURE PRESERVE

Located in the park's most northern section, the preserve can be accessed by hiking the Bluestem Trail. Dedicated in 1970, this 120-acre tract is a remnant of sand hills formed during the Wisconsinan glacial period, which created the Northern Moraine and Lake Region of Indiana. Large amounts of fine sand deposited by glacial outwash streams were morphed by winds into flat sand plains and rolling dunes, as we see in this area today. The well-drained upland areas of the preserve contain black oak and sparse shrub cover, while the lowland areas contain pin oak, black gum, and red maple. Areas that have opened due to disturbance have been taken over by flourishing prairie vegetation. An effort has been made to maintain these prairies to presettlement conditions, using prescribed fire burns and other types of brush control.

Tippecanoe River State Park is one of the few Indiana parks involved with releasing river otters back into the wild.

THE COMPLETE GUIDE TO INDIANA STATE PARKS

The Tippecanoe River is a classic spot for getting out and exploring nature by boat.

TIPPECANOE RIVER NATURE PRESERVE

Dedicated in 1975, the 180-acre preserve is located along the river near the center of the park, with access along the Oxbow Trail. Trail 4 passes through the southern section of the preserve, and Trail 5 passes through the northern section. Silver maples, cottonwoods, and black willows are most common in areas subjected to frequent flooding, whereas the drier areas have red oak and black walnut. The swamp oxbow sloughs are especially attractive to water birds, such as great blue herons, which also

A camp is nestled into the shaded woods of Tippecanoe River State Park.

have a nesting colony in a remote area of the state park. Other birds frequenting this area include wood ducks, green herons, kingfishers, and red-headed woodpeckers. Many mammals such as deer, muskrat, beaver, and mink frequent the area. Due to its remoteness in the park, the preserve also serves as a location for river otter release.

TEPICON HALL RECREATION BUILDING

Situated on the west end of a clearing in the northern section of the park, Tepicon Hall is nearly all that remains of Camp Tepicon. Built of native materials, the historic recreation building is a beautiful, intact example of the craftsmanship that once existed on the property in the 1930s. The T-gabled building is primarily constructed of timber frame with exposed support beams. Built by the WPA around 1938, it is listed on the National Register of Historic Places.

Other amenities include 112 camping sites with electric, 56 primitive horseman's sites, 10 sites for canoe camping, and rental cabins.

One of the most popular activities is boating down the Tippecanoe River in a canoe or kayak; 11 miles of river are within the borders of the park. The park also has as much adventure in its woods as it does on the water—offering 10 hiking trails from easy to moderate, totaling over 22 miles. The park's southern section is a convoluted group of looping hiking trails that connect to one another at various points, most of which are also multiuse for hiking and horseback riding. Few state parks accommodate horses as much as hikers, but in Tippecanoe River State Park, many of the trails sprawling through the park's southern section are shared by both.

TRAIL 1—SAND RIDGE TRAIL—HORSE/HIKING

(1.8 miles) Moderate—A conglomerate of four looping paths connected together, the trail begins near the fire tower parking area or waterfowl parking lot, and it leads to the fire tower while traversing sand hills and marshy areas. Located just southwest from the campground, the trail connects to Trail 2 along its northern section and Trail 6 along its southern portion.

TRAIL 2—PIN OAK TRAIL—HORSE/HIKING

(4.7 miles) Easy—Located along the western edge of the park, the trail is made up of two loops connected by a long, winding center trail. Horses may start from near Fire Tower Road while hikers might find the best access point from the campground. The trail leads through oak forest and along some open fields, snaking around private property and sand hills.

TRAIL 3—HOMESTEAD TRAIL—HIKING

(1.5 miles) Easy—A short connecting route looping north to south, the trail begins north of the campground entrance, heads north to a railroad, and then returns to park road. While leading through oak forest, pine plantation, and open fields, the path crosses both Trail 5 and Trail 4.

TRAIL 4—OXBOW TRAIL—HIKING

(2.3 miles) Easy—The trail loops from the campground to the playfields and main picnic area, leading along Oxbow Lagoon, through low river bottoms, along the river, and back up into the pines and fields, while passing through the Tippecanoe River Nature Preserve. The trail connects with Trail 3 at its western section and connects with Trail 5 while north, inside of the Tippecanoe River Nature Preserve.

TRAIL 5—RIVER BLUFF TRAIL—HIKING

(4.3 miles) Moderate—The trail begins north of the campground passing prairies, river bluffs, and oak woods. The trail may be hiked from the canoe camp, north of Trails 3 and 4, or from the Potawatomi Group Camp or Rent-A-Camp area, connecting Tepicon Hall in the northern section of the park to the Tippecanoe River Nature Preserve.

TRAIL 6—THE BARRENS TRAIL—HORSE/HIKING

(2.3 miles) Moderate—Made up of three connected loops, the trail is located in the central part of the collection of southern hiking trails. The trail leads through oak forest and open fields and then returns to the horse camp, with connected access to Trails 1 and 9. It begins north of the horse camp, crosses the main road along the marsh, and leads north up into sand hills.

TRAIL 7—WHITE PINE TRAIL—HORSE/HIKING

(2.9 miles) Moderate—The path is a series of connected loops that lead through the western section of the park, with a horse entrance spur trail leading north to the park office. The path connects with Trail 9 along its southeastern section. It covers flat woodlands, open fields, and pines.

TRAIL 8—BLUESTEM TRAIL—HIKING

(1.4 miles) Moderate—This short, looping trail is located in the northern tip of the park. The path begins at the Tepicon Hall parking area, with the northwestern section of the trail passing through the Sand Hill Nature Preserve. While starting out as a large stand of pine trees, the trail predominantly turns into a large swath of prairie grasses and oak woods.

TRAIL 9—BLACK OAK TRAIL—HORSE/HIKING

(2.0 miles) Moderate—Located in the southern edge of the park, the path begins on west edge of the horse camp and circles west through oak woods and sand hills. While traveling northwest along the southwestern edge of the park, the trail connects to Trail 7.

TRAIL 10—SAND BLOWOUT TRAIL—HORSE/HIKING

(1.1 miles) Moderate—East of the horse camp and day-use area, the path circles through a small section in the southeast corner of the park, predominantly consisting of prairie and sand blowouts. The trail connects with Trail 9 leading directly west.

12

Versailles State Park

Established 1943—5,988 acres

1387 US 50 East

Versailles, IN 47042

(812) 689-6424

39.08, -85.23

Versailles State Park is the second largest state park in Indiana, and while layered in beautiful woodlands, it also has some of the richest Civil War and battle history in the state. Between July 8 and July 13, 1863, John Hunt Morgan and 2,000 cavalrymen known as Morgan's Raiders made their way through the southern Indiana area, taking control of the town of Versailles.

In August 1934, commissioners of Ripley County were given the task of creating a county park board in order to direct and secure everything needed to establish a federal park in Ripley County. By October, the Department of Interior announced that they had acquired 1,700 acres of submarginal land unfit for profitable farming from farmers north and east of the town of Versailles. While many cabin foundations from these farmers can still be seen today, the Dieckman Family Cabin was of particular importance at the time, as it was used as the first headquarters for the Versailles park project. Then known as Versailles Federal Park, it was estimated that the first federal park in Indiana would cost $100,000 to $300,000 for the development of the area for recreational purposes. Work began immediately on October 2 with the park road from the Busching Bridge to the Dieckman Farm improved for increased traffic.

The area was designated the "Versailles Recreation Demonstration Area," and responsibility for development of the property's facilities was turned over to the Civilian Conservation Corps (CCC). By January 1935, the area was settled by 200 young men in Company 596 with the orders to construct 15 barracks, a mess hall, an administration building, and a recreation building. Other facilities constructed by the CCC include a fire tower, the Oak Grove Shelter, and Group Camp 4. An additional 65 acres called Hassmer Hill were donated by Hassmer, along with a house to be remodeled into a 4-H Camp. With both the CCC and the Works Progress Administration working on the project, the 4-H Camp was hurried in order to be ready for the first 4-H campers in July 1936. While the camp was a success, the house burned down in 1955, the camp was officially closed in 1977, and all of the buildings were demolished.

While the area was mostly clear-cut and devoid of trees, massive tree plantings by the CCC, as well as an on-site tree nursery, helped the landscape flourish, reverting back to mostly forested woodland. When not working, the young men were given opportunities to improve themselves through educational courses as well as sports teams. The CCC lived and

A statue of a Civilian Conservation Corps worker memorializes the hard work done by the CCC in the 1930s.

worked on the property until 1937 when they left to work on other projects in Oregon. In honor of their service, Versailles State Park dedicated a CCC commemorative statue in 2010.

Both the Winamac and Versailles Recreation Areas were turned over to the state of Indiana in April 1943, and the name was officially changed to Versailles State Park. After years of interest in the property, the state was essentially handed a completed park with a proven history of successfully serving the public—complete with a campground, picnic and shelter areas, a fire tower, and two group camps. By the 1970s and after

A sun sets on the horizon of Versailles Lake.

a long run of recreational activities, the park was in desperate need of substantial repair. Along with revitalization, the park added a saddle barn in 1960 and a new gatehouse and another campground in 1970. Today the park totals 5,988 acres.

Rock quarries were built within the park's borders to supply the needed material to construct many of the park's structures and roads. The Oak Grove Shelter originally constructed by the CCC was built using stone from an on-site quarry as well as native timber. It remained the only shelter in the park for 45 years until five new shelters were constructed in 1988.

Construction of Versailles Lake began in January 1954, using prison laborers to construct a 230-acre lake in four years. The lake resides within a 169-square-mile watershed, with tributary waters, such as Laughery and Fallen Timber creeks, continuously feeding the waterway. Laughery Creek is named in honor of Revolutionary War soldier Col. Archibald Lochry. In 1781, while traveling down the Ohio River to meet with George Rogers Clark at the Falls of the Ohio, Lochry and 32 of his men were ambushed, captured, and killed in a battle with Native Americans at the location where Laughery Creek enters the Ohio River, just south of Aurora.

While swimming is not allowed in Versailles Lake, a swimming pool complex, complete with a waterslide, has served swimmers since 1987,

The Busching Covered Bridge is a historic landmark to Versailles State Park.

when the swimming beach was officially closed. Fishing and boating continue to be a few of the most popular attractions at Versailles State Park.

The bright red bridge located just before the park's gatehouse is known as the Busching Covered Bridge and was built in 1885 by Thomas Hardmen. The bridge is 176 feet long, 15.5 feet wide, and 16.5 feet tall. The bridge was the main entry point into the park until 1930 when a new road was built. Today, the bridge is still operational, sprawling across Laughery Creek, and is used as a shortcut into the town of Versailles by many visitors.

The comfort stations for the campgrounds were originally constructed of stone and wood by the CCC in the 1930s, and 226 campsites within Campgrounds A, B, and C offer electric, with a camp store open in the summer months. Campground A was also constructed by the CCC and is the oldest campground in the park, located in an area of heavily wooded rolling terrain. Campground B was later constructed by the Division of State Parks in 1975. Campground C is the newest addition to the park.

The southern and central parts of the park nearest to the park's entrance consist of moderately rated hiking through thick overgrown forest. While only three hiking trails exist, they lead through some of the most beautiful forested areas in Indiana, crossing over Fallen Timber Creek several times before climbing up steep hills to a vista overlooking Laughery Creek. The numerous ups and downs can make hiking portions of the park extremely difficult while along the Old Forest Trail. However, both the Orchard Trail and Fallen Timber Creek Trail are rated as easy, offering visitors a peaceful ramble through the heavily forested landscape.

TRAIL 1—OLD FOREST TRAIL

(2.25 miles) Rugged—Made up of one large looping trail, the path winds through the southern section of the park past ravines, large notable sinkholes, and along the eastern bluff of Laughery Valley. With only a thin layer of topsoil covering the limestone bedrock, rainwater has exposed several sinkholes, typical of the karst topography of the area. The southern tip of the trail can be accessed by taking Fire Tower Road to its dead end, and the northern tip can be accessed at the CCC-constructed Oak Grove Shelter. While large portions of the park had once been cleared of trees, the section where the path travels is one of the few places with old-growth white oak and beech trees dating back to the 1840s.

TRAIL 2—ORCHARD TRAIL

(2.75 miles) Easy—Consisting of two looping trails that make a figure eight, the western loop circles Campground A, while the eastern loop is located immediately north of Campground B. The land surrounding the trail was once the homesite of Eliphalet Stevens and his wife Margaret. Near what is now the Oak Grove Shelter and Campground A, the Stevens family established a working orchard. Produce from the orchard was carried by ox to the town of Madison, where it was sold and put aboard ships along the Ohio River. Sadly, a cholera epidemic struck the area in 1852, killing four of the Stevens's children and many neighbors on what is now park property. Victims of the outbreak were buried in a remote, closed cemetery inside the borders of Versailles State Park.

TRAIL 3—FALLEN TIMBER CREEK TRAIL

(1.5 miles) Easy—Beginning north of Fallen Timber Bridge, the path runs east, hopping over Fallen Timber Creek and attaching to Trail 2 (Orchard Trail). Along the trail near the second creek crossing, a leading citizen in the Versailles area known as Leander Webster once had a cabin. The trail is what remains of the old horse and buggy road that passed the cabin, and large flat rocks used to construct the road can still be seen today. Also owning a sawmill operation, Webster floated his logs from his mill down Fallen Timber Creek, south into Laughery Creek, and then into the Ohio River. The road that once passed the cabin where Webster died in 1895 leads east from Versailles past the Pleasant Hill Cemetery where Webster is buried.

MOUNTAIN BIKE TRAILS

Only a few of Indiana's state parks are lucky enough to have extensive mountain bike trails, and Versailles State Park is a prime example of the benefit these trails offer mountain bike enthusiasts. Maintained by the Southeastern Indiana Mountain Bike Association, their website gives the most up-to-date information on all mountain bike trails within the park, along with detailed information about specific trail specs like elevation change and path grades.

TRAIL 1—GRANDVIEW LOOP

(6.0 miles)—Like the other trails at Versailles State Park, Grandview Loop can be ridden in either direction. There are rocks and technical parts, but this ride is characterized by its climbs and its descents. You have two choices: Ride it counterclockwise and reach the long, flowing downhill first. Then a bit later, do the climb, which is a rocky service road section that isn't a whole lot of fun (but is relatively short). Your other option is to ride it clockwise and have a rocky service road descent, which is followed by a longer grind uphill. If you want a fun downhill, I say ride it counterclockwise. If you are doing hill workouts, then do it clockwise. On hot summer days, you'll notice that the trail can be breezy and comfortable on top of the bluffs, yet stifling in the valleys. It will make you want to work hard to find the breeze again.

TRAIL 2—CENTER LOOP

(2.0 miles)—There are two ways to reach Center Loop. The easiest would be to follow the intermediate Creekside Loop. Alternatively, you could reach this loop by following the more difficult Cliffside Trail. Ride it in either direction as a lollipop loop to head back to the trailhead, or to add distance, ride onto a larger loop of the trail system and link to Grandview Loop. Look for some rocks and a bit more climbing as this trail goes higher on the bluffs.

TRAIL 3—CREEKSIDE LOOP

(1.4 miles)—This trail connects Center Loop, Grandview Loop, and Turtle Loop together. It is essential for riders doing Grandview to ride some portion of this trail. Its biggest characteristic is its rocks. There are a lot of them. Most of them are decomposed chunks of limestone, fist-sized or smaller, but there are also larger slabs of limestone for good measure. Keep on the lookout for optional lines to add technical challenge for more advanced riders. This section of trail might convince you to leave the micro-knobby race tires at home and instead use something with a little more grip.

TRAIL 4—CLIFFSIDE

(2.5 miles)—This trail is the second left off of Shadow Run at the apex of the first big switchback (if riding Shadow Run clockwise). It begins with a good bit of exposure high on the bluff above Laughery Creek. It is kept technical, with rocky sections, before it heads into the forest on its way toward Center Loop. Keep your eyes peeled for cool rockwork (there is a great bench for two constructed from rock) and optional technical features like skinnies.

TRAIL 5—TURTLE LOOP

(1.0 miles)—This lollipop loop is the easiest in the park. If you're a new rider, take a left shortly after you begin Shadow Run to head down this trail. It's not technical, and there are no big climbs like on Shadow Run. You can go either direction around the loop at the end and return to the trailhead, or if you're more adventurous, you can try the rest of Shadow Run next. At the tip of the lollipop loop, Creekside branches off. Creekside is a moderately difficult trail, primarily because of the rocks and the short, steep sections. It will lead you to Grandview and Center

Loop. Many riders do a counterclockwise loop and finish their ride on Turtle Loop.

TRAIL 6—SHADOW RUN LOOP

(3.8 miles)—All rides start here. This trailhead begins across the street from the swimming pool parking lot. In the summertime, the pool is a great spot to cool down after a hot ride. There is a kiosk and a few picnic tables in the shade nearby, also. You have to begin on this trail to reach other parts of the trail system. Riding this loop counterclockwise gives you a steeper climb with a few switchbacks, but it gives you a long, straight downhill to finish. Ride it clockwise and that long, straight downhill becomes a long grind uphill, and those steep switchback climbs become a more technical descent. Ride it counterclockwise if you're a newer rider or want a faster downhill. Once at the top of the bluff, this trail winds through the forest with relatively little elevation change, hence its beginner rating. There's nothing terribly technical about this trail, but keep your eyes peeled for evidence of the karst landscape (hint: sinkholes!). Some of them are right along the trail.

13

Shades State Park

Established 1947—3,541 acres

7751 S. 890 W.

Waveland, IN 47989

(765) 435-2810

39.94171, -87.091677

Before settlement occurred in the area that would become Shades State Park, Native Americans lived among the forest and treacherous terrain along Sugar Creek. Legend has it, a Piankashaw Miami village existed within the borders of the park, while groups of the Shawnee and Kickapoo are also thought to have passed through the vicinity. With European development taking over the area, the Miami tribe eventually ceded the land to the federal government in 1818. Since the land was of little value to farmers due to the rough terrain, the forest was spared and avoided being clear-cut for agriculture.

While the property was originally known as "The Shades of Death," no one really knows for certain when or how it earned its name. Haunting legends of Native American attacks and lovers' quarrels have painted a grim picture of the area, while the deep ravines and dark hemlock groves continue to give rise to superstitious fears. While it is said that the name has referred to the way the thick forest canopy tends to block out the sun, the land is painted with the dark history of several murders that were known to have occurred in the 1800s on what is now state property. In 1836, Moses Rush was killed by his wife with an axe—an act that

Steep ravines lead down to Sugar Creek, a popular route for canoe camping in the summer months.

was later decided to have been in self-defense. In 1865, a questionable issue of inheritance money led Milton Wineland to shoot his father and cousin before being killed himself while fleeing down the Wabash River. No matter the reason for the name, the area continues to contain a great amount of risk, with dark, vast ravines cutting through the landscape.

While the way the trees cast their shadow on the ground may have contributed to the property's superstitious legend, it is also the reason the area provides a unique habitat for many plants and animals. The cool sandstone ravines create an environment that allows plants known to exist in ranges farther to the north—such as the Canada Yew, eastern hemlocks, and white pines—to thrive here. Other species such as black locust, sassafras, and eastern red cedar did not exist on the property prior to an original survey in 1819, yet they exist today due to sections of the land being clear-cut for farming and then allowed to succeed back into forest. Wildlife abounds throughout the park, which is home to a vast collection of field birds. Turkey vultures also visit the park using thermal updrafts created from the park's sun-warmed cliffs.

CCC AND CAMP SHADES

Between 1935 and 1942, the Civilian Conservation Corps (CCC) Company 2579 made the property their home, setting up their camp at a place they called Camp Shades. While the Shades Inn health resort was still in operation and the park was yet to be established, eight acres were leased from Joseph W. Frisz to the CCC for their camp in order to construct four barracks, a mess hall, shower building, and an area for a water tank. Projects completed by the CCC include the impoundment that created the large pond, dams on streams, and organized tree plantings. When Indiana was first settled in the early 1800s, little was known about erosion or soil conservation. A major task of the CCC was to supply the property's farmed areas with erosion control and fertile topsoil. The camp remained for many years after the CCC left the property, but it was eventually dismantled in 1951.

THE DELL HOUSE AND SHADES HEALTH RESORT

As early as 1819, surveyors first noted that mineral springs existed on the property deep in the land's ravines, and by 1863, the area had become a popular destination for Wabash College students. In 1886, the popularity of using springwater for medicinal purposes was booming, and cool, fresh water on the property led to the land being quickly purchased by the Garland Dells Mineral Springs Association. A year after purchasing the land, the association built the Dell House to serve as a health resort, and the entire property was developed into a healthful recreation area named "The Shades."

In 1901, state geologist W. S. Blatchley noted three springs on the property. Joseph W. Frisz, known as "The Father of Shades," purchased stock in the Garland Dells Mineral Springs Association in 1909 and eventually bought out his partners, gaining complete control by 1914. While Frisz's motives were environmental as well as entrepreneurial, he was adamant about preserving the property and saving the land's trees, often diverting road construction in order to avoid cutting any trees on the property. Frisz spent the next 15 years keeping the natural area under preservation, while continuing to buy more land, building the land stock to 2,200 acres. The area became a popular attraction for hikers and swimmers, with the perk of natural spring water. By 1929, the resort included an already existing 40-room inn built in 1886, 14 cottages, and a pavilion with theater and dance hall. As the property prospered, many of the park's locations of interest, such as Silver Cascade Falls, Maidenhair

Autumn color lights up the forest at Shades State Park.

Falls, Pearl Ravine, and Inspiration Point, were named during the height of the health spa's operation.

SAVE THE SHADES

Following the death of Frisz, his family decided to sell the land, but they were unable to find a buyer who could promise to preserve the land. In 1947, Baxter Foundation bought the land and held it until public funds could be raised for state purchase. A public crusade organization called "Save the Shades, " spearheaded by the American Legion, began raising the money needed to buy the property. The American Legion contributed $79,608 toward the campaign, and Indiana's schoolchildren raised $11,500 in small-change donations. With the combined efforts of donation boxes from banks across the state, Montgomery County citizen contributions, and large private individual donations, $262,000 was eventually raised. On April 16, 1948, when the land was officially saved as Indiana's fifteenth state park, 10,000 people showed up to the dedication ceremony.

Today, the park encompasses 3,082 acres and has as many as 11 springs on the property. After the health spa declined in operation, and the land found its way into the hands of the state, the inn continued to be used until 1965. It was eventually torn down in 1968 due to the cost of maintenance and repair. The pavilion, long used as a place for delight and dancing, came to the same fate as the old inn in 1981 when high repair costs gave the Department of Natural Resources a reason to tear down the old structure and give Shades State Park a more natural setting. The former inn and pavilion once stood where the Dell Shelter and the picnic area currently reside.

THE DEVIL'S PUNCHBOWL

A notable key landmark of the park, Devil's Punchbowl, was first named by early settlers around the same idea that the property had demonizing characteristics. The large circular sandstone formation was originally cut out by small streams, creating high canyon walls and an unusually dry natural setting that has been a drawing attraction for generations.

ROSCOE TURNER AIRSTRIP

Dedicated to recognize all of the pioneers in civil and military aviation, the Roscoe Turner Airstrip was dedicated by Indiana's Department of Conservation on September 18, 1960. The 3,000-foot-long, 120-foot-wide

Waters flows down into a canyon at Shades State Park.

turf strip was used for light aircraft, and at one time was the only airstrip located in a state park. However, while memorial plaques and signs remain to mark the historical landmark, the airstrip was permanently closed in 2002.

DEER'S MILL COVERED BRIDGE

Once common throughout the state, covered bridges were designed with a covered roof in order to protect the wooden structural integrity and minimize maintenance. Constructed in 1878 by Joseph J. Daniels, the 275-foot bridge has been preserved as a historic relic. Today, the bridge is closed to motorized traffic, since State Road 234 was redirected over Sugar Creek in 1968. The double-span bridge is maintained as a historic attraction and is open to pedestrians to explore. The bridge is named after Joel Deer, who in 1829 operated the area's first millhouse and had a hand in developing a now-vanished community.

PINE HILLS NATURE PRESERVE

Located on the eastern edge of the park is the Pine Hills Nature Preserve, a 470-acre preserve dedicated a National Natural Landmark in 1968 and Indiana's first nature preserve. The property protects deep canyons formed by the tributary waters of Indian Creek as it drains into Sugar Creek. The property was given to the state of Indiana by The Nature Conservancy in 1961 and was officially dedicated in 1969. Most of the area is rich in pine species, planted with white pine, Scotch pine, Jack pine, as well as Norway spruce. Once inside the borders of the preserve, by way of Trail 10, and after crossing over State Road 234, a 1.6-mile trail leads through five inimitable features. The preserve's crown feature is a 100-foot high ridge, barely the width of a hiking trail, known as "Devil's Backbone." Additionally, four other main trail sections divide the property into what are known as Turkey Backbone, Woolen Mill and Mill Cut, The Slides, and Honeycomb Rock. The trail section of Woolen Mill and Mill Cut once contained Pine Hill Woolen Mill Company built in 1870. A water-powered mill designed to spin thread from raw wool, the operation failed and was moved just three years after construction. Today, no historical artifacts or evidence exists from the old mill except for the U-shaped notch in the stone of Mill Cut Backbone. The area past the Woolen Mill and Mill Cut is known as The Slides due to the large amount of loose stone from rock slides, created from the repeated freezing and thawing of the surface rock. The last key feature of the preserve

Icicles form on the rock faces of the lower bottomlands at Shades State Park.

is Honeycomb Rock; an Upper Mississippian Age formation made up of sandstone and fossilized algae, it is thought to have broken off from the sheer eroding walls that line the trail.

The park prides itself on being old-fashioned, and current overnight accommodations remain in the dark ages by choice. Camping sites haven't offered electricity since opening in 1989, and the 104 of them are divided between Rookery Ridge, Raccoon Run, Whitetail, and Locust Grove camping sectors. However, a modern shower house exists, and the campground is notoriously quiet, especially during the week. The campground also offers a playground, water fill station, dumping station, and easy access to most of the hiking trails in the park by way of the Campground Loop Trail.

Canoe camping is available down Sugar Creek approximately two miles downstream from the Deer's Mill Bridge. The area is one large, open campsite, big enough for seven groups but specified for two tents and six people per site. Only primitive camping is allowed, and arrangements with Shades State Park must be made prior to camping on a first-come, first-serve basis. Shades State Park is unique in offering canoe camping and is only one of three in the state that offers such an experience, the other two being Tippecanoe River State Park and Chain O' Lakes State Park. Canoe rental is available near the Deer's Mill Covered Bridge along with a canoe launch ramp just northeast of the bridge. A 12-mile canoe trip will lead visitors to the Brush Creek Ramp takeout point just before Narrows Covered Bridge near Turkey Run State Park. A 16-mile canoe trip stretches to the Cox's Ford Bridge, just past Turkey Run State Park to the west. While parking is limited to a 15-minute unloading zone at the Brush Creek Ramp, there are five permitted parking spaces available at the Cox's Ford Bridge. Contact the property office to inquire about these parking permits.

Seven backpack sites exist and can only be reached by using the 2.5-mile Backpack Trail. Each site offers a picnic table, fire ring, access to potable water, and a vault toilet. This feature is truly unique to Shades State Park, as no other park in the system has a camp specifically designated as a backpack site. Sitting high on a bluff overlooking Sugar Creek, the site is said to be one of the darkest camping spots in the park, allowing visitors to view the nighttime sky in an incomparable setting.

TRAIL 1—DEVIL'S PUNCHBOWL TRAIL

(0.75 miles) Moderate/Rugged—This short, loop trail passes the Hickory Shelter and leads to two overlooks of Sugar Creek: Prospect Point and Inspiration Point. Another interesting feature of the trail is a nice view of Silver Cascade Falls. Silver Cascade Falls is a convex waterfall, unique in that it flows down the rock face in a convex formation instead of over a cliff's edge. This unique attribute prevents freezing and thawing that normally splits apart the lower rocks below.

TRAIL 2—LOVERS' LEAP AND PEARL RAVINE TRAIL

(1.25 miles) Rugged/Very Rugged—Starting at the Dell Shelter, the trail leads to a split, which either heads north to Sugar Creek or south, looping back to Sugar Creek after passing Maidenhair Falls, Pearl Ravine, and ending at Steamboat Rock. The trail gives access to a spur trail leading to Lovers' Leap on the western section. An excellent view of Silver Cascade Falls, Canoe Island, and Sugar Creek can be had from an observation deck built out over the cliff called Lovers' Leap. Steeped in legend, Lovers' Leap is merely a beautiful spot with a wooden overlook that allows visitors a perfect view of the glimmering waters below. The spur trail is one-way and must be retraced in order to return to Trail 2.

TRAIL 4—FRISZ RAVINE TRAIL

(0.625 miles) Moderate/Rugged—The trail starts at the Hickory Parking Lot and makes a loop down to Sugar Creek and back. The west section of the trail is moderate, while the east section traverses up and down a series of ladders through the area's steep ravines. The trail connects with Trail 5 on its eastern section and Trail 7 on it southwestern section.

TRAIL 5—KINTZ RAVINE TRAIL

(0.75 miles) Moderate/Rugged—Similar to Trail 4 in length and design, the path traverses through steep ravines and loops to Sugar Creek and back. The path leads through Kintz Ravine, with a ladder on its western section.

TRAIL 6—RED FOX RAVINE TRAIL

(0.5 miles) Easy—This short connector trail leads through Red Fox Ravine; it connects to Trail 1 on its northeastern end and Trail 9 on its southwestern end.

TRAIL 7—KICKAPOO RAVINE TRAIL

(0.875 miles) Rugged—This challenging, looping trail can be accessed from Trail 4 from the east or Trail 8 in two locations from the west. The western section passes through Kickapoo Ravine.

TRAIL 8—SHAWNEE CANYON TRAIL

(0.75 miles) Rugged—Similar to Trail 7, the path is accessed from the east by way of Trail 7 or from the Backpack Trail in its southwestern section. The northern tip of the trail parallels with Sugar Creek and leads west into Shawnee Canyon. The trail then leads south through a creek bed and ends at a crossroads that allows hikers to either hike to the campground, follow the Backpack Trail to the west, or hike to a connector trail leading back to Trail 7 to the east.

TRAIL 9—CAMPGROUND CONNECTOR TRAIL

(0.5 miles) Easy—This Y-shaped trail connects the parking area near Dell Shelter and a large pond to the youth tent-camping area to the south, as well as leading to the park road to the west.

TRAIL 10—PINE HILLS CONNECTOR TRAIL

(1.5 miles) Moderate—This long, stretching trail connects the Dell Shelter to the Pine Hills Parking Area to the east and then continues onward to the Pine Hills Nature Preserve farther east.

BACKPACK TRAIL

(2.5 miles) Moderate—The trail connects the Hickory Parking Lot to a backpack camp located in the westernmost section of the park. The path passes connections with Trail 8 twice before reaching the park's campground area and Campground Loop Trail, and before continuing west to the backpack camp, which is located above Sugar Creek.

14

Whitewater Memorial State Park

Established 1949—1,710 acres

1418 S. State Road 101

Liberty, IN 47353

(765) 458-5565

39.613889, -84.965278

The area encompassing Whitewater Memorial State Park has an often forgotten historical significance: it was used by Native Americans as a prime hunting ground, and it also became one of the first areas to be settled. When European settlers first arrived in the area, they encountered the Miami, Delaware, and Illinois tribes. By 1795, the resident tribes were forced to relinquish their claim to the land in the Treaty of Greenville, resulting from their loss during the Battle of Fallen Timbers. While most of the territory drawn out in the treaty became southern Ohio, a smaller portion of land was taken over by the state of Indiana, including what is now the Whitewater Memorial State Park and Brookville Reservoir.

The park's land was purchased by the surrounding counties of Union, Fayette, Franklin, and Wayne as a memorial to the men and women who served in World War II. The park became the sixteenth park in Indiana's state park system in 1949—with part of the property bordering Brookville Lake, which is leased from the Army Corps of Engineers.

The project began to take form in 1945 when residents from all four counties created the Whitewater Memorial Park Association. The group's main task was to raise funds to purchase the park's first 1,800 acres along

A pair of sandhill cranes fly over Whitewater Lake.

Silver Creek. With the Department of Conservation approving the site, other local conservation clubs pushed to promote the project as much as possible, eventually acquiring 1,512 acres four years later. Labeled as a living memorial to the counties' men and women who served in war, the official dedication was a patriotic affair at the location of a soon to be constructed dam. The construction of the earthen wall dammed the waters to create a 200-acre body of water named Whitewater Lake. Since officially opening to the public in 1953, Whitewater Lake and many of the other man-made water features surrounding the property have made fishing and boating the primary activities at the park.

Construction of Brookville Lake began in 1965, and the reservoir began operating in 1974 to control flooding in the Whitewater Valley. The lake is a municipal water supply for the region and is stocked with channel catfish, striped bass, muskellunge, walleye, largemouth bass, white bass, black crappie, bluegill, rock bass, smallmouth bass, rainbow trout, and brown trout. Other fish species include carp, gizzard shad, white sucker, minnows, and darters. The Whitewater River is said to be the swiftest river in the state, declining in elevation an average of six feet per mile.

A large patch of trilliums flourish
throughout the forest floor.

A horsemen's camp and a long, looping horse trail make Whitewater Memorial State Park a popular place for horse riders.

NATURALIST CABIN

During the 1970s and '80s, the naturalist cabin was the set for the popular television program *Indiana Outdoors*, filmed in Indianapolis. The cabin was later transported to Whitewater State Park near the campgrounds and beach.

Shoreline hiking, flat-water boating, swimming, fishing, and camping opportunities are abundant around the 200-acre Whitewater Lake—with access to Brookville Lake and other recreational facilities. Brookville Lake provides many opportunities for seeing migrating flocks of birds. The forest at the time of first settlement was still wild, hosting woodland bison, cougar, wolf, and black bear. Flocks of passenger pigeons—with numbers in the hundreds of thousands—were also flying through the woods. Since turkeys and eagles were also common, a reintroduction project released turkeys, white-tailed deer, and bald eagles back into the area. Today, the land is used to preserve wildlife, and the large bodies of water provide a safe haven for migrating birds.

HORNBEAM NATURE PRESERVE

Located along the western shoreline of Whitewater Lake, the 83-acre Hornbeam Nature Preserve was dedicated as an example of mixed hardwood forest typical to the area of Indiana. While the well-shaded woodland is a mixed mesophytic forest, the understory also includes an unusually high number of large ironwood and blue beech trees, combined into one category known as hornbeams, which gives the preserve its name. The preserve is located on Ordovician sandstone, shale, and dolomite. Glacial deposits from both Illinoian and Wisconsinan glaciers covered the area. Fossils have been exposed where streams have cut down through the bedrock.

TRAIL 1—MEMORIAL TRAIL

(2.5 miles) Moderate—One of the more centrally located trails, the path can be accessed at many places near most of the park's popular picnic areas. The trail passes the naturalist cabin used for interpretive programs as well as the amphitheater, Poplar Shelter, and South Shelter, before crossing the Bridle Trail along the eastern section of the park.

TRAIL 2—CATTAIL ALLEY

(1 mile) Moderate—The path connects the middle section of the campground to the beach and bathhouse along the northeastern shoreline of Whitewater Lake, traveling east to west.

TRAIL 3—RED SPRINGS LOOP

(1.2 miles) Rugged/Easy—The trail begins at the entrance sign to the Hornbeam Nature Preserve and follows an easy dirt path southeast to Whitewater Lake spillway. Crossing the road, the trail descends steeply downhill and becomes rugged, passing a large wooden deck that provides a good view of the red seep spring that gives the trail its name. An out-of-this-world sight to see, the reddish tint of the water comes from the iron and minerals carried in the water, providing a unique habitat for plants and animals.

TRAIL 4—LAKESHORE TRAIL

(2.75 miles) Moderate—The trail begins at the parking area used for the entrance to Hornbeam Nature Preserve and leads northeast along the edge of Whitewater Lake one-way for 2.75 miles. A short half-mile trail exists near the trail's starting point and serves as a short loop through the northern section of the Hornbeam Nature Preserve.

TRAIL 5—VETERANS VISTA LOOP

(2 miles) Moderate—Winding through upper hillside forests and lower wetland fields, the trail is a mixture of soft-surface dirt and a mown-grass pathway. The narrow hiking trail is predominantly well shaded and provides a good view of the lake, especially in the autumn when the leaves have fallen. Starting at the parking area for the Silver Creek Boat Ramp, the trail leads swiftly uphill to the east where a small wooden picnic structure exists at 0.14 miles from the parking lot. The path travels uphill, crosses the park road twice, and then descends along Brookville Lake—crossing over several wooden platform bridges at 0.29, 0.43, 0.56, 1.03, 1.28, and 1.49 miles before looping back to the west side of the parking area.

BRIDLE TRAIL

(9 miles)—The long path traverses the entire outer edge of the park's property—looping from the horsemen's day-use area on the west side of the park to the horsemen's campground in the eastside. Two smaller loops exist near the Memorial Trail and the park's entrance.

15

Chain O' Lakes State Park

Established 1960—2,718 acres

2355 E. 75 S.

Albion, IN 46701

(260) 636-2654

41.333056, -85.380556

Between 13,000 and 14,000 years ago, massive ice sheets advanced across the land. In what would become northern Indiana, the Wisconsinan ice sheet and the Erie and Saginaw Lobes carved and molded the land into a series of depressions and ancient riverbeds. These depressions, known as kettle lakes, formed as large pieces of ice broke away, became partially buried, and then melted to form small lakes. Large mound formations known as eskers were formed as glacier meltwater escaped through cracks in the ice and then deposited sand, silt, and gravel into upside-down stream beds.

Once home to a Native American tribe, a camp consisting of 30 bark wigwams was located along the north shore of Bowen Lake—previously known as Indian Lake—prior to official European settlement. The first settlement by a white man occurred with the construction of a home along the same north section of Bowen Lake by William Bowen who arrived in the 1830s. Once other settlers arrived, forests were cleared and the area became farmland. While some of the cleared wood was used for fences and buildings, most was burned.

The idea to create Chain O' Lakes State Park first began in 1937 after the Department of Conservation conducted a survey to locate a potential

Chain O' Lakes State Park is a paddler's dream, as many of the lakes can be accessed by connected streams.

state recreation site in the area. After 10 years, the Department of Conservation's lead planner, Donald Johnston, recommended the site as "a natural lake state park," and legislation soon appropriated a starter fund and approved to levy a tax for Allen, Whitley, and Noble counties to raise the additional $250,000 needed. Progress was briefly halted after an injunction was filed by citizens unhappy with the tax increase, and the funds were held in escrow until 1956. After a few months, the

White trilliums cover the forest floor.

legal complaints were finally dismissed, and the Chain O' Lakes Joint Park Board purchased the land the following December. Land acquisition began with the first 50 acres of the park, located west of Long Lake, purchased from Mr. and Mrs. Harrison Finster. In 1959, an additional $300,000 was approved to purchase the final tracts of land and begin developing the park. By the following year, close to 1,400 acres had been acquired. On Sunday, June 12, 1960, the park was officially dedicated as Indiana's fifteenth state park. When the park celebrated its twenty-fifth year and silver jubilee on June 12, 1985, the park was rededicated with a plaque and stone anniversary marker, which still reside on the grassy hill next to Sand Lake Beach. The park has continued to expand over the years, and in 2012 the property had grown to 2,718 acres containing 13 natural lakes.

As the name suggests, the park is a paradise for water lovers, with 9 connecting lakes and 13 lakes total. Bowen Lake reaches the deepest depth of 65 feet, while Dock Lake only reaches to 20 feet. The lakes are designated electric motor only, to enhance the quality of the lake's canoeing experience.

THE STANLEY SCHOOLHOUSE

The Land Ordinance of 1785 designated that the sixteenth section of each township must be set aside to support a school. After Indiana became

The Stanley Schoolhouse at Chain O' Lakes State Park is on the National Register of Historic Places for its significance in history and for its architecture.

a state in 1816, Indiana townships often sold the section and used the proceeds to build a school. The one-room Stanley Schoolhouse was built in 1915 and held simultaneous classes for grades one through eight until 1947 and for grades four through six until 1954. The school was named for the landowner Henry Stanley and is the fourth to exist on the property. The current schoolhouse structure is brick, preserving it through the ages. The classroom has the original blackboard, roll-down maps, and desks, as well as the original bell tower. The area around the schoolhouse also contained an outhouse, water pump, and schoolyard for recess. The building functioned as a schoolhouse until it closed in 1954 when schools were consolidated into Green Center School. After operation ceased, the building remained vacant until the Tri-County Park Board purchased the land to be added to Chain O' Lakes State Park. More recently, the schoolhouse served as the park's nature center from 1978 until 2012. The schoolhouse has been fully restored and was added to the National Register of Historic Places in 2014.

Other buildings with historic significance exist throughout the park, including the Department of Corrections building located in the most eastern section of the park in a part of the Glacial Esker Nature Preserve. Still used today, the building, built in 1967, was originally used as a youth rehabilitation dormitory, whose youth often did work throughout the park. The Sand Lake Bathhouse was constructed in 1971, and the park's campground gatehouse, originally constructed in 1973, was torn down and completely rebuilt in 2006.

THE INDIANA TRAIL 100

The first race of its kind in Indiana, the ultramarathon traverses through Chain O' Lakes State Park by way of a 100-mile and a 50-mile course. The race must be completed in 30 hours for the 100-mile course and 15 hours for the 50-mile course. The race is organized by the Indiana Trail 100 nonprofit, with net proceeds given to Chain O' Lakes State Park.

GLACIAL ESKER NATURE PRESERVE

Dedicated in 2012, the 732-acre preserve was established to protect the glacial features in several key sections of the park. Formed by glaciers, the topography of the preserve areas includes flat-bottom lowlands cut by glacial meltwater, creating areas with shallow wetlands, creeks, and floodplain forests. Large glacially deposited stones known as "Erratics" remain scattered throughout the tracts surrounded by upland forests along the ridgetop and ravines. Due to the large collection of interconnected kettle lakes, the area is abundant with wetland and forest interior plants and animals dependent upon large, unfragmented wetland and forest ecosystems. Notable animal species—including the brown creeper and the hooded, cerulean, and prothonotary warblers—are found in this preserve, which is also home to several hawks, barred owls, and great blue herons.

NATURE CENTER

Once housed in the Stanley Schoolhouse until 2012, the nature center is now located in the Sand Lake Beach House, and it offers visitors interpretive programs, live animals displays, and an opportunity to read about the history of the park. Native American artifacts hang on the walls, including arrowheads dating back to 1000 BC.

FAMILY CABINS

The family cabins were constructed between 1978 and 1979 and are surrounded by thick, shady woods. Indoor woodstoves offer visitors a warming experience, and all cabins feature a master bedroom with a double bed and a second bedroom with two bunk beds. Each cabin is 850 square feet, and includes a spacious living area, full kitchen, and a bathroom with shower.

A shaded trail at Chain O' Lakes State Park.

CAMPGROUND

The original 360-site campground was built by youth rehabilitation boys in 1966. Today the park offers 331 sites with electric, 49 sites without electric, 33 primitive sites, 4 Rally Campsites, youth tent camping, and a canoe camp.

TRAIL 1

(1.5 miles) Moderate—The trail begins north of the campground, follows a ridge through the woods before dropping down in a valley, crosses two channels as it circles around the north side of Dock Lake, and returns to the campground.

TRAIL 2

(1 mile) Moderate—This trail begins at the parking lot on the north shore of Bowen Lake, follows the lakeshore through the woods, and returns to the parking lot.

TRAIL 3

(1.3 miles) Easy—The trail starts and ends at the Sand Lake Beach and loops south past the Sunny Shelter and Shady Shelter. An additional part of the trail connects the campground with the beach.

TRAIL 4

(1.5 miles) Moderate—This trail connects the youth group tent camp and Rally Camp to trails that wrap around Sand Lake and lead to the swimming beach. It crosses between Rivir Lake and Mud Lake and passes the canoe camp area.

TRAIL 5

(1.3 miles) Easy—The trail loops around Sand Lake, beginning and ending at the Sand Lake Beach House. It connects with Trail 4 on the west edge of Sand Lake and Trail 7 at two locations along the north shore of Sand Lake.

TRAIL 6

(3 miles) Rugged—A loop trail south of Dock Lake, it enters the Glacier Esker Nature Preserve along the trail's eastern section, with an option to continue on to the park's rental cabins, past Sucker Lake, and back. It connects with Trail 1 twice along the trail's northern section and connects to the family campground along the southern section of the trail as well while returning from Sucker Lake.

TRAIL 7
(1.8 miles) Easy—This looping trail begins and ends at the Sand Lake Fishing Pier, covering the area north of Sand Lake. It partially enters Glacier Esker Nature Preserve along the trail's eastern section, connecting with Trail 2. The path also connects with Trail 5 along its southern section near Sand Lake.

TRAIL 8
(0.5 miles) Moderate—This trail loops around the larger and western of the two Finster Lakes known as Big Finster Lake. It accesses the Stanley Schoolhouse along an eastern spur trail and Trail 1 along the trail's western section.

TRAIL 9
(0.75 miles) Rugged—This trail begins in the parking area across from the Stanley Schoolhouse and leads east through the Henslow's sparrow restoration area open field, through a wetland, and onward to a looping path that circles Kreiger Lake and returns back to the trail leading back to the parking area.

TRAIL 10
(2.5 miles) Moderate—This large loop trail south of the campgrounds is cut into two sections. There is a connection to Trail 6 just east of the campground.

TRAIL 11
(4 miles) Easy—This trail connects the Stanley Schoolhouse and the youth tent / Rally campgrounds. This turf-covered trail is excellent for cross country.

TRAIL 12
(3.5 miles) Moderate—This trail begins and ends at the beach. It travels through glacial topography and hardwood forest, and it follows the ridgeline of a deep ravine featuring a meandering stream.

16

Ouabache State Park

Established 1962—1,104 acres

4930 E. State Road 201

Bluffton, IN 46714

(260) 824-0926

40.72, -85.11

Indiana's famed buffalo trace was a pathway between Falls of the Ohio and Vincennes in southern Indiana. While wild bison were gone from Indiana by the 1800s from overhunting, Ouabache State Park celebrates the legacy of the native animal by housing a small herd of bison within a 20-acre enclosure.

These bison represent the herds that once roamed Indiana and have been a popular park feature for decades. Earlier exhibits included many other animals, resembling a small zoo, but today only domesticated bison make the park their home.

Before the state park was established, the previous 996-acre property was known as the Wells County State Forest and Game Preserve and was widely acclaimed as "the greatest wildlife laboratory" in the United States. It was during this era sometime in the 1930s that a small collection of animals, including a live bear, mountain lion, eagle, coyote, fox, and badger were exhibited within the property's main attraction called the Vermin House. While operating as a game preserve, they supplied over 425 conservation clubs with young game birds while also turning out roughly 3,500 pheasant eggs and 1,800 quail eggs on a daily

The perfect spot for a lakeside picnic.

basis. Raccoons and rabbits were also raised for release before the game-raising program was phased out, and the property officially became the Ouabache State Recreation Area in 1962.

This change switched the property management from the Department of Natural Resources Division of Fish and Wildlife to its Division of State Parks. Having undergone many changes since first being used by the state, the property was officially designated a state park in 1983, and it currently manages 1,104 acres. Pronounced "Wabash," the park's name comes from the French spelling of a Miami Indian word "waapaahšiiki," meaning "water over white stones," referring to the river that forms the southwest boundary of the park. Over time, however, locals and visitors who have grown up with the park pronounce the park's name much differently, some calling it "Obachee." Additional confusion transpired from an incorrectly spelled Indiana Department of Transportation sign, advertising the park as Quabache, which remained unchanged until 1997, leading people to call the park "Quabachee." Today it is common practice by even park staff to sometimes pronounce the park's name differently than originally intended.

An up-close-
and-personal
view of one
of the bison
that makes
Ouabache State
Park its home.

CCC

The area was once covered in a dense forest of hardwoods before settlers clear-cut the forest, farmed the land, and turned the property into a harsh environment of abandoned scrubland. When the Civilian Conservation Corps (CCC) arrived on the property, very few trees even existed, and reforesting the landscape quickly became one of their most engrossing tasks. They were also responsible for building a 110-foot fire tower, which remains one of only two surviving towers in northern or central Indiana State Parks. While the CCC is credited with building most of the park's structures, their efforts on the lodge recreation building, with its original hardwood floors and interior maintained in near-mint condition, make the lodge one of the brightest gems the park has to offer.

A statue near the entrance of the park was placed in 2014 in memory of the young men who served in the CCC. The statue honors the men of Company 1592 S-93, who served at the property.

HORSE AND BUGGY PARKING

The park has special accommodations for horse and buggies used by the local community, particularly members of the Amish community from the nearby town of Berne, Indiana. The special parking area is provided because horses are not allowed to travel throughout the park.

FIRE TOWER

The fire tower is currently closed and being restored by the Friends of Ouabache State Park with an estimated cost of $75,000. As time passes, many of these old fire towers have become lost to disrepair or deemed too dangerous for visitors.

PARK AMENITIES

The park offers boat rental near the shore of its 25-acre Kunkel Lake. The six-mile "Ouabache Trail" circles the entire park, leading past the bison enclosure, through old-growth forest, past historical buildings and every ecological environment that exists in the area. Totaling 13 miles of soft-surface pathways, the trails intermingle at points and showcase all that Ouabache State Park has to offer. Other amenities include a paved biking trail connecting to the famed Rivergreenway Trail, a 15,000-square-foot beach with a swimming area on Kunkel Lake, as well as tennis, basketball, and volleyball courts. One hundred twenty-four

A historical fire tower reflects
in the waters of Kunkel Lake
at Ouabache State Park.

The sun rises on Kunkel Lake at Ouabache State Park.

electric campsites are split between two campgrounds: Campground A with 77 and Campground B with 47.

OUABACHE FLATWOODS NATURE PRESERVE

Located in the central section of Ouabache State Park, this 38.16-acre tract is a part of the Bluffton Till Plain Section of the Central Till Plain Natural Region. Primarily consisting of an oak flatwoods ecosystem, the relatively level terrain and poorly drained soils aid in the area being dominated by large specimens of swamp white oak, burr oak, and pin oak, with a diversity of tree species including black walnut, American beech, Ohio buckeye, black cherry, and several species of hickory. The forest is considered old second growth, and it is the highest quality forest remaining in Wells County.

Almost three miles of a paved bike path lead through the park and connect with two additional miles outside park property, connecting Main Street with the White Bridge in the town of Bluffton. Originally the path was the old Indiana 316 road, and it is the only bike path–town connector trail of its kind in Indiana's state park system.

TRAIL 1—BISON EXHIBIT TRAIL

(1 mile) Easy—This smooth, semi-gravel path circles the bison exhibit, giving visitors a glance at every angle of the 20-acre enclosure.

TRAIL 2—CONNECTOR TRAIL

(1.5 miles) Easy—This trail connects Trail 3 and Campground A to a looping path that passes between the swimming pool and tennis courts and over a footbridge in the northeastern section of the park.

TRAIL 3—CAMPGROUND LOOP TRAIL

(0.9 mile) Easy—A looping trail leading from Campground A, it heads directly east before ending back near the campground. The northern trail section connects with Trail 2, while the southern trail section connects with Trail 5.

TRAIL 4—CONNECTOR/LAKE TRAIL

(3 miles) Moderate—This trail branches off of Trail 1 near the bison enclosure and winds west to connect with Trail 5 before looping around the south-central part of the park and connecting with a Trail 4 lake loop.

TRAIL 5—THE OUABACHE TRAIL

(6 miles) Moderate—The longest trail in the park is accessed at many points throughout, as well as from most of the other hiking trails. The trail passes by all of the key features the park has to offer.

TRAIL 6—PAVED BIKE PATH

(2.68 miles) Moderate—This paved path runs along the western edge of the park and connects the southern section of the park to the Rivergreenway off park property. The path is designed for visitors interested in a longer bike ride, opting to take advantage of an additional 2.5 miles of biking out of the park along the Wabash River.

17

Harmonie State Park

Established 1966—3,465 acres

3451 Harmonie State Park Road

New Harmony, IN 47631

(812) 682-4821

38.06, -87.95

The area is unique due to the nearby town of New Harmony, where two groups moved to live an experimental, communal life. The Harmonists of the Rappite Community, immigrants from Wurttemberg, Germany, first settled in Pennsylvania around 1804 before moving to the Indiana Territory—purchasing 30,000 acres of heavily forested land and building a town on the banks of the Wabash River in 1814. Led by Father Johann George Rapp, the group settled in the area to escape religious oppression and to live out what they believed were the last days of life on earth.

Because the area had a geological structure similar to their previous home of Harmony, Pennsylvania, the group was familiar with using the natural materials of clay, sandstone, and limestone to build their new Indiana town—as well as the ample timber and fertile soil, which helped the town become self-sufficient and thrive. By 1824, 180 structures had been built, including a brick church, a granary, all four community houses, and a sawmill. When the group decided to move back to Pennsylvania in 1825, the town was sold by Father Rapp to a wealthy Scottish industrialist named Robert Owen.

Owen and his financial partner, William Maclure, a well-known geologist of the time, dreamed of establishing a town where education

The Wabash River runs along the western border of Harmonie State Park.

and social equality would prosper, helping not only the people living within the town's borders but also the entire world. By inviting some of the greatest scientific and artistic minds to experience the community they had built, Owen and Maclure set out to establish the settlement as a world-renowned hub of progressive thinking and a center of science. While a large number of people passed through and worked in the town, many famed creative minds visited, including American naturalist Thomas Say, French naturalist and artist Charles-Alexandre Lesueur, French educator Madame Marie Duclos Fretageot, Dutch geologist Gerard Troost, and feminist Frances Wright. The rocks and rapids of the nearby Wabash River provided important paleontological and zoological discoveries, as well as serving as the perfect natural setting for artistic creativity. While the town never grew to the size Owen and Maclure had hoped, New Harmony was a center for progressive education, as well as scholarly and scientific research, until the Civil War and was best known for its headway in education, women's rights, and architecture. From the development of such a progressive-thinking community grew the first free public school offering equal education for boys and girls, the first free public library, and the first kindergarten in the United States. While Owen left in 1827, his family and the scientists and educators that followed him remained—continuing to make outstanding contributions to the community and the state of Indiana. Key historical features remain in the town, including a replica of the original Harmonist Labyrinth, a concentric circular design constructed out of circular hedges and planted according to a pattern established by the Harmonie Society. A Harmonist Cemetery exists near West Street and holds the remains of 230 members of the Harmonie Society, buried in unmarked graves. Also within the walls of the cemetery are the mounds of Woodland Native Americans dating back to AD 800. Today, New Harmony remains a small but culturally rich town with enough historic sites to satisfy a whole day of exploring.

The property that would become Harmonie State Park started from a simple memorial gift of 700 acres given to the state of Indiana by the two daughters of Elmer E. Elliott from Spencer, Indiana. The Elliott family ties reach back to the Owen era of New Harmony, and their land was once a part of the original 30,000 acres purchased by Robert Owen. Due to Elliott's deep interest in conservation and his desire to see the land used by the people of New Harmony, as well as his two daughters' involvement with many facets of preservation and revitalization of Indiana, the land was officially dedicated in 1966.

Thought to be the "biggest drawing card in the Midwest," development of the park was continually held up due to disputes over land acquisitions and lack of funding. As of 1972, with only 3,000 of a proposed 4,200 acres purchased and one mile of roadway and parking lots for two picnic areas built, the property was used only sparingly for primitive camping. After two years, funding improved, and by 1974 the state approved $2 million to hasten construction of the then 3,400-acre Harmonie State Park. Thanks to a grant from the United States Bureau of Outdoor Recreation totaling $763,000, funds would be split between Harmonie, Spring Mill Lake, and Clifty Falls for use in the construction of Olympic-sized swimming pools—with Harmonie State Park's pool completed and named in honor of Elmer E. Elliott in August 1978.

Today, the property boasts 3,465 beautiful acres, with its name stemming from the old German spelling for the town of New Harmony and the Harmonie Society. It offers 200 electric campsites and 11 modern cabins. Known today as Cabin 4, the first prototype cabin was constructed with the help of park staff in 1989, with 10 more built by Arc Construction Company and dedicated August 30, 1991. Costing $6,100 each, the cabins were built with a rustic design using white pine logs from Clark State Forest that was split by the nearby Department of Corrections. Each cabin offers a wood stove, electric heat, and air conditioning, as well as all of the modern conveniences.

Six park shelters have been built, some dating back to the 1970s. The Hilltop Shelter, Tulip Shelter, Pecan Shelter, Big Oak Shelter, Cherry Hill Shelter, and Sycamore Ridge Shelter all have their own functioning purpose within the park while resting on their own unique parcel of land. The Hilltop Shelter, Tulip Shelter, and Pecan Shelter are all centrally located to the park's key recreational features near the park's entrance. The Cherry Hill Shelter is the central location of the short, looping path of Trail 6 and is surrounded by the Harmonie Hills Nature Preserve, while the Sycamore Ridge Shelter is nestled directly in the heart of some of the best mountain bike trails in the area.

The nature center is situated right in the heart of the campground, giving campers convenient access to interpretive programs and a wealth of knowledge on the wildlife and history of the park. Several live animal displays allow visitors a chance to get a closeup view of several snake

Harmonie State Park is one of the only state parks to still have an active oil-pumping operation within its borders. A refurbished antique oil pump has been set aside as a monument to the area's historical oil industry.

species, as well as an exceptional beehive housed behind glass between the nature center's walls—covered with doors that resemble real tree bark to give the appearance the bees are living in a real tree. A large window offers visitors the opportunity to catch birds feeding in the garden behind the center, and the walls are covered with a large collection of animal mounts. The mounts include a Canada goose and gosling, raccoon, wild turkey, and many more, as well as a buck, coyote, and collection of bass in the park's office. Each of the park's 11 cabins also displays a wonderful fish mount.

The discovery of oil in Indiana during the early twentieth century helped the area of New Harmony to prosper, and the evidence of these pumping operations still exist around and within the borders of Harmonie State Park. Oil drilling first started in Indiana around 1890 with approximately 50,000 wells, but only 12,000 or fewer are currently active today. When the land for Harmonie State Park was originally gifted to the state of Indiana, mineral rights were retained and leased to private companies—a practice that continues to this day. The first oil well on the property was 2,382 feet deep and completed December 9, 1945. Since that time, over 50 wells have been drilled within the state park borders, extracting millions of barrels of oil between 1957 and 1983.

Most of the wells were originally owned by the Sinclair Oil Company, later purchased by Ashland Oil and Atlantic Energy, and then taken over by Charles M. Brandenburg, who bought them in 1988. As the wells were officially declared abandoned in 1991 after Brandenburg's permit was revoked, the Indiana Department of Natural Resources and the D.K. Parker Co. were left to clean up at least six wells leaking at the surface, eventually plugging 43 abandoned wells using the money from a forfeited $30,000 bond Brandenburg lost by abandoning the wells.

Today, only a few wells continue to operate on the property with remains of past operations scattered throughout the park, including several saltwater injection pumps that can be seen along the park's main road. An old pump jack stands in front of the swimming pool parking lot as a monument to the area's rich history of oil extraction.

WABASH BORDER NATURE PRESERVE

Encompassing 255 acres, located along the northern border of Harmonie State Park, the Wabash Border Nature Preserve contains a mature dry-mesic upland forest, mesic ravine forest, and wet floodplain forest bordering the Wabash River. Many rare and notable species have been identified in the area. Receiving very little human interaction, the remainder of the preserve continues to be highly protected.

HARMONIE HILLS NATURE PRESERVE

Located in the southern section of Harmonie State Park, the 335-acre tract contains one of the largest collections of mature mesic upland forest in the Southwest Lowlands Natural Region. Several rare fish species are found in the area's small waterways. The forest contains species of plants and animals that are area-sensitive forest interior creatures, dependent upon large, unfragmented forest ecosystems.

The southern section of Harmonie State Park has two distinct trails designed for mountain biking, but they are used by hikers and trail runners as well. Mountain Bike Trail 1 is rated for beginners and is four miles long, while Mountain Bike Trail 2 is rated for experienced riders and is over six miles in length. Created in 2008, the trails were designed and built by the Hoosier Mountain Bike Association with help from the Indiana Department of Natural Resources. Trail maintenance is supported from the Evansville Mountain Bike Association, and new trail construction is an evolving process.

Wooden walkways and bridges direct hiking paths across the fishing ponds at Harmonie State Park

Over seven miles of hiking are available along seven trails. Aside from a few steep descents into some of the park's ravines, the hiking in the park is easy to moderate, leading through a landscape that was once farmland. Old structures like barns still exist within the woody thickets of the forest, yet today very little evidence of farming can be seen. The trails at Harmonie State Park are lush and vibrant with activity from the park's ponds, creeks, and rocky scenery.

TRAIL 1

(1 mile) Moderate—This trail is a reasonably easy loop path connecting two different sides of the youth tent area, down a ravine and up through lush woodlands and grassy plateaus. The trail allows access to the park road several times along the northwest section and allows hikers an easy connection with two mountain bike trails in the southwest and Trail 4.

TRAIL 2

(1.5 miles) Moderate—The trail begins from either end of the campground and travels through wooded hills and down into a small stream, making a loop that returns to the opposite end of the campground. The trail is perfect for allowing campers access to most of the longer trails in the park and the toughest terrain.

TRAIL 3

(1 mile) Moderate—The trail overlooks a small stream and includes a rather steep hill, making a loop from the Poplar Grove Picnic Area. Many shelters are located within close proximity of the path, making it a great trail for groups using the picnic areas. The northern section briefly passes through the Wabash Border Nature Preserve and passes a water tower.

TRAIL 4

(2.5 miles) Moderate—The longest trail in the park crosses two streams and travels up and down a steep ravine, winding along the borders of the heavily forested Harmonie Hills Nature Preserve. The trail can be accessed only by using one of the other nearby trails such as Trail 1, Trail 2, or from the mountain bike parking areas in the southern section of the park.

TRAIL 5

(0.75 miles) Easy—This is a good trail for observing pond wildlife or the chewed trees left by beavers. Located near the campground gatehouse, the trail leads over a large collection of wooden stairs and bridges around Little and Big Harmonie Ponds. A great fishing location, the ponds are stocked with bluegill, sunfish, bass, and catfish and reside just a short walk from the cabins. While mostly a wetland experience, parts of the trail heading back to the campground gatehouse follow a wide grassy path leading to a parking lot or into the campground. With such a large amount of water year-round, the trail remains lush and vibrant with shade-tolerant plant species. In the warmer months, dragonflies graze over the waters, and the evening air is full of the songs from frogs. Alive with insect activity, bats can be seen hovering across the waters just after sunset, keeping the insect population in check. Big Harmonie Pond is home to large aquatic turtles as well as the largest concentration of bullfrogs and green frogs in the entire park.

TRAIL 6

(0.75 miles) Easy—This short and sweet trail runs though the east section of the Harmonie Hills Nature Preserve. The trail is a loop and can only be accessed from the Cherry Hill Shelter at the picnic area.

TRAIL 7

(1 mile) Easy—This short walk leads to a small loop and the Edmonds Cemetery. Named after Henry Edmonds, the cemetery contains the graves of two of his three wives—his first wife, Elizabeth, who died in 1847, and his third wife, Sarah Axton, who died in 1853. While no other markers are present, it is believed by members of the community that 21 to 30 other people are buried in the cemetery around a large cedar tree. About a mile from this location and off park property is Goad Cemetery, where many of the Edmonds children and other relatives are buried. Henry Edmonds died May 14, 1863, at the age of 82 with no record of his burial location to be found.

RIVER WALK

(0.25 miles) Easy—Winding along the Wabash River and near the boat launch and Wabash River Picnic Area, this short path leads along the edge of the shore past old, rusted signs and washed-out floodplains. The area is a wide-open mini-park, complete with playground and lots of thin woodlands to explore.

J. C. EGLI MEMORIAL BLUEBIRD TRAIL

The trail is named in honor of J. C. Egli, the first vice president of the volunteer organization Friends of Harmonie State Park, who was instrumental in getting the project started in 2012. Currently, there are over 37 bluebird boxes taken care of by volunteers. The trail follows through the edge of a large field, where the bird boxes are scattered throughout.

18

Potato Creek State Park

Established 1969—3,840 acres

25601 State Road 4

North Liberty, IN 46554

(574) 656-8186

41.552547, -86.348065

During Native American times, plants with potato-like roots, such as sweet flag and Jerusalem artichoke, grew along the creek banks and were collected as a food source. Early settlers' English translation for the name the Native people gave these potato-like plants was "wild potato," which in turn gave the area its name of Potato Creek. The name was officially referenced during one of the area's first surveys by D. Hillis in 1834, and he frequently described the creek as rapid, noting that rapids existed where the park lake is today. Once settlers arrived, water continued to be a principle characteristic for survival, as Potato Creek was used at least six times for powering sawmills and gristmills. It is no wonder that the waterway became so popular for mills, since it drops an average of three feet per 5,000 feet, totaling a 150-foot drop in elevation throughout its span. Before a dam was constructed to form a lake, the area was often stricken with flooding from Potato Creek, as many of the groundwater springs fed into it.

Darcey Worster and fellow conservation club members first proposed the creation of an artificial lake in the 1930s by damming Potato Creek; however, engineers speculated that the area would never sustain a lake. This became a challenge for Worster to prove otherwise.

Tuberous plants growing along the
edge of Worster Lake have helped give
Potato Creek State Park its name.

Worster continued to work on the project independently, drawing his own maps and taking soil core samples while also sending handcrafted insects to state officials to "bug" them about creating the lake and a state recreation area. After extensive research was conducted by the Indiana Department of Conservation, it was announced on June 27, 1939, that the dam would be built using Works Progress Administration workers, but progress on the project was immediately halted with the start of World War II. The project gained steam once again in 1964, when Robert J. Fischgrund spoke at a session with the St. Joseph County Committee for Recreational Development, making the suggestion that $1 million be raised to finance Potato Creek State Park. With $2,250 from the committee, a feasibility study was conducted and found that the site had "clay pan" subsoil, making it a sufficient site to construct a lake. However, when the committee held a public meeting for the local people of North Liberty, 150 people turned up, many of whom were strongly opposed to the project. Once made up of 110 different properties, the old farmland was used for agriculture, poultry farming, and six maple sugar camps.

With such a strong farm history to the area, the local landowners were afraid of losing the farms and barns that generations had spent building. After attempting to find another location, two additional sites were proposed, but the Department of Natural Resources eventually settled for the Potato Creek area after opposition had ceased. Turmoil seemed to continue for the next few years, fighting permitting and land acquisition, until approval for Potato Creek State Park was officially announced by Director John Mitchell on March 22, 1968. The project faced its final setback after Governor Edgar D. Whitcomb was elected and development work ceased until January 30, 1970. Actual conversion of the farmland to a park occurred when Raymond Fisher arrived to live on the property in the summer of 1971, clearing away old buildings, salvaging materials, and seeding the sites with grass. Salvageable buildings were auctioned off and several old farmhouses were moved just down the road from the park. After development was completed, the state park opened and after three years of operation, it was formally dedicated on June 6, 1977. At the time of opening, the entire project had cost the state of Indiana $5.7 million to acquire the necessary land and develop all of the park's property and facilities—including Worster Lake, a family and horsemen's campground, a youth tent area, hiking and horse trails, a paved bike path, beach and bathhouse, the picnic shelters, and the park's visitors' center. By 1979, the park ranked third in visitation in the entire state park system, only beaten by Brown County State Park and Indiana Dunes State Park. Today, the park encompasses 3,840 acres.

State Representative Richard Mangus made a difference for Indiana's Natural Resources and the people who enjoy them by successfully advocating for the development of many of the recreational features at Potato Creek State Park. During his 32 years spent in the Indiana General Assembly, his efforts helped fund the bike trail, cabins, trails, picnic areas, campgrounds, a nature center, and the interpretive naturalist services. The park remembered his public service by honoring him with a plaque at Potato Creek State Park.

WORSTER LAKE

With Potato Creek already a popular swimming hole by the turn of the century, it is no wonder the abundance of water in the area inspired Darcey Worster to first suggest the building of a lake. A self-taught

Potato Creek State Park is a popular destination for mountain bikers.

naturalist and woodsman, Worster was a native of the town of North Liberty and spent much of his time roaming the area prior to the establishment of the park. While Worster worked for over 44 years to make his lake dream become a reality, he passed away on November 11, 1974, never seeing the lake. The 327-acre Worster Lake is named for Darcey Worster and is still mostly water fed from Potato Creek, which continues to be connected to many groundwater springs. Two miles long, the lake's average depth is 10 feet and it is highly prized for fishing all year-round, with ice fishing when the lake is frozen.

VARGO HILL

The eastern section of Potato Creek State Park is particularly rugged. Vargo Hill stands 885 feet above sea level, with a southern slope known as Steamboat Hill. Southeast of Vargo Hill is Cullar's Hill.

THE HUGGART SETTLEMENT

One of the first free African Americans to settle in the area was Samuel Huggart, after he purchased 80 acres of land in St. Joseph County in 1834. Over time he was joined by many other families, who intermingled and worked side by side with their white neighbors during a time when slavery still existed. Andrew Huggart, the brother of Samuel, arrived in 1840 and became a prominent figure, becoming superintendent of the Union Sunday School while serving as a journeyman. By 1860, the farm settlement was prosperous with planted crops and maple sugar and had increased to 160 acres. Other people who lived in the community included members of the Manuel, Bass, Boone, and Powell families, with the settlement reaching its peak around 1890. The community is best known today for defying Indiana's settlement law before the Fugitive Slave Law was passed in 1851. They built a one-room schoolhouse for both blacks and whites, who socialized in one another's homes and worshiped together at the local Olive Branch church. Many members of the Huggart Settlement were buried in the Porter Rea Cemetery, where the old Fryar Mill once stood.

THE PORTER REA CEMETERY

Many cemeteries from old landowners and organizations have often become a part of state park property. The Porter Rea Cemetery is unique among the others having racially integrated burials. The cemetery was officially created on September 6, 1854, when Samuel Gard deeded the land

The incredible glow of autumn colors.

to trustees for a burial ground. Free African American settlers from the Huggart Settlement were buried there alongside their white neighbors. The Porter Cemetery Association was formed in 1884, with both African American and white charter members. The first burial to have occurred was nine-year-old Emma Porter in 1845. Since then the cemetery has had several names, including Porter Burial Ground, Porter Grave Yard, and the Porter Cemetery, before gaining its current title. Rea was added to the name honoring another local family. The cemetery is active today and contains over 600 burials; it is managed by the Porter Cemetery Association. When the park acquired that land during the establishment of Potato Creek State Park, an earthen levy was constructed west of the cemetery to protect the graves from high water. Historical features of the cemetery include a water pump used to draw water for plants, stone borders that define family plots and carriage paths designed for narrow horse-drawn buggies and a horse-drawn hearse. The cedar tree is a key fixture of the old cemetery, as it was a symbol to the Victorians of everlasting life. This is why many of the oldest cedars are in the same location as the oldest graves. The cemetery received a historical honor on September 13, 2003, when a historical marker was placed at its entrance by the Indiana Historical Bureau.

SCHRADER SPRINGHOUSE RECONSTRUCTION

It was once common practice to build springhouses over natural flowing springs in order to take advantage of the abundant source of water, which historically remains a constant 50 degrees Fahrenheit in Northern Indiana. Built primarily of locally sourced materials, such as stone and wood, the springhouse was also used to store food with jars and cans laid on a cool stone floor or directly in the water. The springhouse at Potato Creek State Park was originally used by Stanton Porter when he purchased the property on March 20, 1837. When the land was later acquired by the Schrader family, it was a part of a 160-acre piece of property that would later become park property. Having decayed beyond repair, the original spring box was removed and rebuilt in 2009 by the Friends of Potato Creek Park. Keeping with historical practice of using local materials, the wood framing and sheathing was from a tulip tree from park property that had fallen in the late 1990s. Today, the building stands as a historical feature of the park, representing life from another era.

SWAMP ROSE NATURE PRESERVE

A constant mission of the park continues to be to return the land to pre–European settlement conditions. Swamp Rose Nature Preserve serves a valuable part of that endeavor and is located along the northeast section of the park. The area offers a glimpse into the slow formation of a wetland and the deer, fox, coyote, and songbirds that make the preserve their safe haven. The preserve contains an area that provides an example of eutrophication, where a lake has slowly filled in, over hundreds of years, to become a wetland. A number of rare plant species are found in the nature preserve. Since no advertised trails travel into the preserve, the area is especially protected from illegal collection and foot traffic.

Prescribed burning of the park's natively planted fields helps control unwanted plant species.

PRAIRIE AND WETLAND RESTORATION

The first efforts to restore the fields to presettlement conditions began around 1991. While prior managers of the park allowed the park to develop naturally, a change in management in 1994 led to an intense push toward wetland restoration as well. These projects helped fill in the void of diverse plant management left from previous landowners. Financed mostly by grants and partnerships, 32 wetlands and over 115 acres of prairie have been restored. Native grasses and wildflowers were planted, and drain tiles used to drain the wetlands were broken. During a different era, the land was once part of the largest freshwater marshes in the world, known as the Grand Kankakee Marsh, which spanned 600,000 acres. While farmers and settlement changed all of that by draining the massive marsh, Potato Creek State Park is praised for restoring almost all of the wetlands on the property.

OSPREY NESTING POLE

Also known as fish hawks, osprey are unique wetland birds that primarily feed on fish. While abundant in Indiana in the 1800s, osprey

Potato Creek State Park is one of the few parks in Indiana that promotes the growth of osprey populations.

populations declined across the United States between 1950 and 1970, with no known breeding pairs in Indiana by 1980. The main cause of the swift decline in population was DDT, a harmful insecticide that was banned in the United States in 1973. When this insecticide ran off farm fields and into the watersheds, the birds' main food source became contaminated. In an effort to help save the state-endangered osprey, two osprey pole nests have been installed, which have successfully had multiple nesting pairs. There are also several naturally occurring nests now. Said to be rarer than eagles, 60 young osprey have fledged from Potato Creek State Park. The osprey that make Potato Creek State Park their home leave the park in late summer, overwintering in warmer, southern climates, and return by mid-March. Osprey imprint on the area in which they hatch and usually return to the same place they were born to raise their own young.

FAMILY CABINS

Potato Creek State Park offers visitors 17 family cabins, each spaciously designed with an open living space, two bedrooms, a bathroom, a porch, and a kitchen area.

The park offers seven shelters for picnics and groups outings, including the Peppermint Hill Picnic Area, Whispering Winds Picnic Area, Tulip Poplar Picnic Area, Deer Meadow Picnic Area, Orchard Shores West, Orchard Shores East, and the Quaking Aspen Picnic Area. Picnic areas are mostly large, wide-open spaces of grassy fields with partial shade outside of the building structures. The Peppermint Hill Picnic structure is fully enclosed and is the only recreation building with a fireplace. Other amenities include a general store, a tubing hill in the winter, a nature center, a beach, and boat rentals. Seven hiking trails travel through old fields, mature woodlands, restored prairies, and diverse wetlands, totaling close to 10 miles; in addition there are connecting trails and over nine miles of horse trails.

NATURE CENTER TRAIL

(0.1 miles)—The short spur trail was built with memorial contributions in honor of Joann Federer Gardener. The path provides the interpretive staff a trail to use during educational programs. Other key features of the trail include a small farm pond created in the 1950s for livestock, a wooden observation deck near where the trail reaches Worster Lake, and a stone retaining wall made from glacial stones removed from the old farm's fields.

TRAIL 1

(2.2 miles) Moderate—The trail passes by the lake and goes through old fields and young woods. When the park was created, several county roads existed on the property, which were then closed to traffic. One such road, once known as Peppermint Road, makes up part of Trail 1. The road's name referenced a peppermint grove that once grew in an area that is now under Worster Lake.

TRAIL 2

(2 miles) Rugged—The trail traverses the hilliest section of the park; it features rich woods and passes small streams. Accessed from Trail 1, the path leads through the park's northeastern section near the Swamp

Rose Nature Preserve. A section of steps lead up Steam Boat Hill and pass Vargo Hill, returning to Trail 1.

TRAIL 3
(1 mile) Moderate—The trail winds through an upland woodland passing Potato Creek ravine where the creek enters Worster Lake. A small wooden boardwalk sits at the edge of the lake. The looping trail begins and ends at the Quaking Aspen Picnic Area.

TRAIL 4
(2.5 miles) Moderate—The park's longest trail passes the most features of any other trail, leading through a diverse mix of different habitats, along Worster Lake, and passing through thick woods to a wetland.

TRAIL 5
(1 mile) Easy—The trail circles through an old field and has a small observation deck at the edge of a small wetland. The trail is accessed from the campground area and is a good, short hike for campers.

TRAIL 6
(0.5 miles) Easy—The trail is a short loop beginning near the visitors' center, leading through a woodland and wetland area. Located in the most southern section of the park, the path is one of the park's shortest trails.

TRAIL 7—FRIENDS TRAIL
(0.75 miles) Easy—The trail is accessed from a small parking area in the park's southwestern section. This loop trail leads through a mixture of partially shaded worn-dirt and mown-grass path, with several observation decks stretching out over a wetland pond.

TRAIL B—BEACH TRAIL
(0.5 miles) Easy—The path is a connector trail, attaching two family campground areas to a spur trail that leads south to the park's beach and bathhouse.

BRIDLE TRAIL 1
(3.35 miles) Easy—Encompassing the entire southeastern corner of Potato Creek State Park, this trail creates a long loop connecting with

the other two bridle trails multiple times. In the southern section of the horse trails area, Trail 1 splits off leading west to the park's gatehouse. At the same intersection, Trail 1 also heads north, wrapping around Summer Pond before passing a small loop and ending back at the horsemen's campground.

BRIDLE TRAIL 2
(1.5 miles) Easy—While this trail does not loop, it connects with Trail 1 several times in order to create a longer ride. Located in the center of the bridle trails, the only access to Trail 2 is either from an intersection south of the campground or by first taking Trail 1.

BRIDLE TRAIL 3
(2.5 miles) Easy—The trail begins at the horsemen's campground, making a short loop just north of the camp, before leading east to create a much longer loop. While circling southwestward, the trail crosses over Bridle Trail 1 twice before returning to the campground.

PAVED BIKE PATH
(3.3 miles) Moderate—The paved path provides a diverse amount of scenery, wrapping around the western section of the park along four distinct sections—the Blue, Green, Red, and Yellow Bike Areas. A west lot along the western edge of Worster Lake provides parking and access to the bike path.

MOUNTAIN BIKE TRAIL
(7.4 miles) Easy—The trail was developed through a partnership between Potato Creek State Park and the Northern Indiana Mountain Bike Association.

CONNECTOR TRAIL
(2.8 miles) Easy—Two long paths that act as shortcuts connect sections of Trail 1, Trail 2, and Trail 4. These paths are the remnants of the area's old roads, used prior to the park's development.

PEPPERMINT LOOP
(0.9 miles) Easy—This short path connects two sections of Trail 1.

19

Summit Lake State Park

Established 1988—2,680 acres

5993 N. Messick Road

New Castle, IN 47362

(765) 766-5873

40.03, -85.3

While the idea for Summit Lake had started as early as the 1950s, it wasn't until 1966 that the park idea began to flourish as the Big Blue River Conservancy District. Known as "Structure 20, Summit Lake," flood control along the river and nearby waterways began in the 1970s, and by 1980 a dam began holding back the water that would become the massive lake. It started as an inspiring personal project of US Congressman Ralph Harvey; he initially helped write the Watershed Act that began the process of funding the project, and he donated the park's first shelter house.

Prior to establishment, the district was thought to be too small for Henry and Rush counties to adequately generate enough tax money to construct a park and maintain it. Therefore, the state was approached to lease the land until it could be arranged to be purchased after attendance proved the park served a purpose. The project was primarily funded by the federal Soil Conservation Service and was intended to be used to control flooding, create a local water supply, and provide Indiana residents near the New Castle area a pristine place for recreational opportunities.

The Big Blue River Recreation Area was sold to the state of Indiana with a lease-purchase agreement of $250,000, and Summit Lake State Park was officially dedicated on January 9, 1988. The park's name derives

The sun sets over Summit Lake.

Many types of wildflowers, such as phlox, spread out in large colonies during the spring season.

from the park's location at the highest elevation in the surrounding area and near the highest elevation in the state.

Historically, the area was mostly woodlands with a small portion of wet and dry prairie in the west. Today, Summit Lake State Park is a combination of an 800-acre lake, thick woodlands, old fields, and wetlands—visited by over 100 migratory bird species. The wetland prairie portions of the property have developed into an important area for waterfowl, and the park boasts of its excellent birdwatching and wildlife observation area. Rare birds find protected resting spaces within Summit Lake State Park as well as Zeigler Woods Nature Preserve located in the southwest end of the property. An abundant array of native flora and fauna thrive

Boating and fishing have been a popular activity at Summit Lake since the park was first established.

throughout the park due to numerous prairie restoration areas. With the lake included, the park manages 2,680 acres.

SUMMIT LAKE

A small watershed mostly covered in natural habitat, the water quality of the lake is mostly clean and clear. With one of the park's main trails leading to shoreline fishing spots, many visitors tend to combine a short hike with fishing. One of the southernmost lakes in Indiana to be counted on to freeze up in winter, Summit Lake has become well-known for its ice fishing. The lake's three small islands help break up the vast waterway, creating several interesting island environments. The area off of Goose Island has historically been a prime fishing spot. Perch Island and Big Island also offer unique fishing and boating experiences.

ZEIGLER WOODS NATURE PRESERVE

Located in the southwest corner of the park, minimal human interaction has protected the first nature preserve in Henry County. Dedicated as a state nature preserve in 1991, the 127-acre tract includes a rolling hardwood forest and wetlands that occur in topographical depressions that once defined the now mostly agricultural east-central part of Indiana. A diverse and mature collection of white oak, northern red oak, white ash, shagbark hickory, sugar maple, and American elm dominate the rich,

Trilliums thrive among the park's semi-shaded forest floor.

wet slopes. On the drier ridges, one will see black oak, basswood, blue ash, red elm, and pignut hickory. Ephemeral wetlands can also be seen during the spring months, which make excellent breeding habitats for smallmouth salamanders and wood frogs.

During the summer months, the park offers interpretive naturalist programs as well as four unique hiking trails. Facilities include 120 electric campsites, three boat ramps, a beach bathhouse, and two large open shelters. Some campsites offer lakeside camping opportunities usually only available at parks with canoe camping. A large swimming beach on the edge of Summit Lake is open from Memorial Day to Labor Day. Two shelters exist in the park: the Sunset Shelter, which gives an amazing view of the setting sun, and the Harvey Shelter.

TRAIL 1—PRAIRIE TRAIL

(2 miles) Moderate—The trail starts in an open field but soon enters some of the most heavily wooded areas of the park. Visitors will pass areas of oak-hickory mixed with cherry, ash, and a beech-maple mix, while meandering a fairly easy path along uplands and low glacial depressions.

Once out of the shaded woods, the majority of the trail traverses open rolling established prairie, with views of the lake. The 60-acre prairie in which the trail circles was once old farmland, and by the time the state officially opened Summit Lake State Park the property was overrun with invasive/nonnative plant species. In 1994 the state mowed and sprayed the field as an initial step to restore the prairie to presettlement conditions. Park staff then planted native grasses such as big blue stem, little blue stem, switchgrass, and Indian grass, along with specifically chosen native wildflowers. Each year between September and April, the state implements a controlled burn on the field to maintain the choice native diversity that has been established. Today, the fields provide not only a living history of what the fields would have looked like before settlement occurred, but they also provide a healthy habitat for a long list of wildlife.

TRAIL 2—CAMPGROUND TRAIL

(1.25 miles) Moderate—The trail begins near the campground in the small oak-hickory woods, with a glacial depression that stays wet year-round. The trail then goes through some scrub growth on the edge of the fields before exiting into open fields across rolling terrain. The trail remains very close to the lake and offers multiple opportunities to view Summit Lake.

TRAIL 3—BEACH TRAIL

(0.9 miles) Moderate—The path begins behind the concession stand at the beach and leads along a gravel path through shaded woods, ending south of the beach in the parking area. The path has a firm and stable surface with less than 2 percent cross slopes and grades no greater than 5 percent, making it the perfect trail for older individuals or those in a wheelchair. Predominantly shaded the entire loop, the path also leads through the central part of the park and provides multiple views of Summit Lake.

TRAIL 4—SELF-GUIDED NATURE TRAIL

(0.75 miles) Moderate—This mowed, grass path leads around a field and through thin woodlands of small trees and shrubs, beginning and ending at the parking area near the Harvey Shelter. Six interpretive stops are marked with wooden posts, and when using the free pamphlet available from the park office, visitors can learn about tulip trees, exotic plant species, wildlife food sources, and many other topics.

20

Falls of the Ohio State Park

Established 1990—165 acres

201 W. Riverside Drive

Clarksville, IN 47129

(812) 280-9970

38.275556, -85.763611

The principal feature of the park is the 390-million-year-old fossil beds located along the edge of the Ohio River. As meltwater from ancient ice-age glaciers carved the Ohio River basin, they exposed fossil beds, providing a unique view of the ancient coral seafloor. Once covered in a shallow tropical sea, these fossils are the remnants of an oceanic life. Among the largest exposed Devonian fossil beds in the world, fossil viewing is allowed but fossil collecting is prohibited in order to preserve the precious site. The waters of the Ohio are at their lowest in August through October, exposing the greatest area of the 220-acre fossil bed.

The Falls of the Ohio was first dedicated as a National Natural Landmark by the National Park Service in 1966. In 1981, the site was designated a National Wildlife Conservation area, providing federal protection to the fossil beds, but no on-site security. The final step to protect the precious resource first began in 1987, when the Clarksville Riverfront Foundation (now the Falls of the Ohio Foundation) formed to raise money to protect the fossil beds and build an interpretive center. Funds were raised through community, state, and federal partnerships. Prior to the establishment of the park, removing fossils was common practice. Today,

The Falls of the Ohio provides a natural setting with the Louisville skyline just on the horizon.

Fossils embedded in the rock create a connection to the past.

the fossil beds are protected by staff with the help of volunteers, while piles of fossil rock from a local quarry sits near the parking lot for those visitors wanting to take home a souvenir.

The Falls of the Ohio have historically been referred to as the Chutes or Rapids of the Ohio, with the term "Falls" dating back to 1742. The actual falls are cascading rapids formed from the river dropping 26 feet over two and a half miles, with an exposed shoreline revealing a graveyard of ancient sea life. More than 600 species of fossils have been identified in and around the fossil beds, with two-thirds of those having been found for the first time in history at Falls of the Ohio. Well over 270 species of birds have been viewed at the park, and John James Audubon made more than 200 sketches of birds while living in the falls area. Over one hundred species of fish have been recorded in the waters, including the primitive paddlefish. Historically, the site was used as a portage point for river travelers when water levels were low. Both low water in the summer and raging torrents of water during the wet seasons have hindered many explorers trying to navigate the river for hundreds of years.

George Rogers Clark Homesite.

One of the park's pinnacle features is the 16,000-square-foot interpretive center, which operates like a museum, with displays about the prehistoric and historic past of the area. The museum features an award-winning movie about the park's exciting history, as well as over 100 exhibits, including "time tunnels." It's often hard to imagine just how old the fossil beds are, but the interpretive center explains in great detail how the large exposure of limestone came to be. This exposure is older than the dinosaurs, and a great deal of emphasis is put on some of the larger and rarest fossils. The wildlife observation room behind the lobby gives visitors an opportunity to view the birds and mammals that visit. While always an impressive educational structure since first being constructed in the 1990s, the interpretive center reopened in January 2016 after a $6 million renovation.

While Falls of the Ohio State Park consists of 165 acres, part of the property is within the 1,404-acre National Wildlife Conservation Area. Located at the lower end of the park is the George Rogers Clark Homesite, known as "Clark's Point." The general lived there from 1803 to 1809. Since Clark's original cabin was destroyed in 1854, a representation of Clark's home was built in 2001 on a seven-acre tract. Another cabin

Driftwood and debris washed up along the shore of the Falls of the Ohio is worn smooth, creating unique scenery.

was constructed next to Clark's to stand in for the home of the McGee family—African American indentured servants of George Rogers Clark. The cabin is representative of a larger community of freed slaves called Guinea Bottoms.

OHIO RIVER GREENWAY

George Rogers Clark Homesite is only a 1.5-mile walk from Falls of the Ohio Interactive Center via the Ohio River Greenway located on top of the levee. The Ohio River Greenway is a 7.5-mile paved path designed for pedestrians and bicyclists to easily travel through Jeffersonville, Clarksville, and New Albany along the edge of the Ohio River and over to Louisville using the Big Four Bridge. The complex project continues to evolve and more information can be found at www.friendsofthe greenway.org.

A highlight of the park is the Gardens at the Falls of the Ohio, which showcases daylilies and many other perennials, shrubs, and trees—all maintained by the park and several volunteer gardening clubs, including Sunnyside Master Gardeners and the Terrace Garden Club. The park's staff and volunteers also maintain summer garden beds around the George Rogers Clark Homesite, with flowers, herbs, and vegetables that Clark might have used.

THE WOODLAND TRAIL AND EXPLORING THE SHORELINE

While the river shoreline offers endless opportunities for roaming, only one hiking trail exists on the property. While advertised as a loop through the woods behind the Interactive Center, parts of the Woodland Trail may be covered with driftwood due to constant flooding. The southern section of this trail travels west along the river's edge and remains more of a wide-open beach of sand and river rock, scattered with spur trails that lead through river brush and into a large maze of fragmented stone cliffs, as the trail itself tapers off near the woods' edge when not maintained. This fossil-rich beach setting stretches in a similar fashion the entire length of the park's shoreline and beyond. The northern section of the Woodland Trail offers an entirely different experience with a gravel pathway and wooden beams outlining the trail edges, stretching into true woodland, giving the trail its name. Wildflowers, patches of river cane, and large trees landscape the path as it travels over two wooden bridges.

21

Charlestown State Park

Established 1996—5,100 acres

12500 Indiana 62

Charlestown, IN 47111

(812) 256-5600

38.43, -85.63

Located on the edge of the Ohio River, the property is a remnant of the jagged "Fourteenmile Creek Valley"—one of the oldest unglaciated stream valleys in Indiana. A tributary of the Ohio, Fourteenmile Creek appears today as a long, twisting lake rather than a creek due to the installation of a group of locks and dams on the Ohio River that periodically raise the water level. The park project was made possible through several donated and purchased parcels from the Indiana Army Ammunition Plant (INAAP), beginning with 859 acres in 1993 and an additional 1,125 acres the following year. The park's recreational facility development began in 1995, and the property was officially dedicated as a state park the following year. In 2004, the park was given an additional 2,600 acres by the INAAP, growing the property to 5,100 acres and making it the third-largest state park in Indiana. Prior to the establishment of the INAAP, most of the land was used for farmland or pasture, but due to persistent forest management and reforestation over 50 years, the area has turned back to heavily forested hills and ravines. Due to the land's natural, rugged design, the scenic area is rich in geological features, archaeological remnants, and concealed habitats for wildlife.

Virginia bluebells form spectacular colonies throughout the moist bottomlands of Charlestown State Park.

PORTERSVILLE BRIDGE AND ROSE ISLAND

At the bottom of a steep, paved hill along the southern section of Trail 3, two very important pieces of Indiana history reside—the Portersville Bridge and Rose Island. Iron truss bridges were regularly built in the United States from 1870 to around 1895, and the restored Portersville Bridge is a relic representative of the time. The bridge exists as a historic landmark and key feature of the park—built by the Vincennes Bridge Company in 1912. Its original location was across the east fork of the White River, spanning between Dubois and Daviess Counties. After being installed only a few weeks, the White River received a record flood submerging the bridge's deck under a few feet of water. Due to damaging debris, the handrails had to be removed, and the bridge was raised three feet in May of 1913. After 86 years of operation, the bridge was closed to traffic in 1999 due to ill repair. With help from several state

The Portersville Bridge connects Charlestown State Park to the historic Rose Island.

representatives, Natural Resource and State Park directors, grant funding from Indiana's Department of Transportation, and the support from the people of Daviess and Dubois counties, the bridge was purchased by Charlestown State Park in 2008, dismantled and relocated to the park. After years of restoration work, the Portersville Bridge reopened as a walking bridge on September 30, 2011, near the same location that the original suspension bridge once spanned across Fourteenmile Creek leading into Rose Island.

While the Portersville Bridge exists as the entry point to Rose Island today, most original visitors arrived by ferry or steamboat along the Ohio River shoreline on the opposite end of the park, or they paid a quarter to walk across the previously existing 400-foot suspension bridge called the "swinging bridge." Three large native stone pillars of the original Rose Island welcome sign still exist at the old entry point along the edge of the Ohio, as well as piers from the original suspension bridge downstream. The large stone pillars along the river's edge held an electric glowing sign that beamed the island's name for miles around. Several steamboats made 90- to 120-minute trips to the island, including the famed *Idlewild* and the largest steamboat at the time, known as *Steamer America*. It is estimated that up to 2,000 passengers took the *Steamer America* steamboat to Rose Island daily. An adult ticket price was just 25 cents, while a child could ride for 15 cents.

Originally established as Fern Grove in 1886, the 118-acre site was once a popular retreat for picnics and church outings, with the Fern Cliff Hotel providing overnight accommodations and an attractive focal point. The property was first purchased by a ferry company in 1886 and converted into a picnic area, becoming a popular stop for the leisure riverboat trips. The pear-shaped peninsula, bounded between the Ohio River and Fourteenmile Creek, was a prime site for recreational activities with a flat, open terrain for picnicking, wooded areas for hiking, and a large 250-foot ridge dubbed Devil's Backbone. While there are many stories of voyagers using the site while exploring the New World, it is known for sure that American settlers who floated down the Ohio on flatboats found the peninsula inviting on hot summer days. At the bottom of the huge ridge, settlers found a cool grove where ferns were abundant and therefore named the modest tract of land Fern Grove.

The resort was purchased by Mr. David B. G. Rose in 1923, who changed the name of the property to Rose Island. Conflicting stories state that the hotel was renamed the Rose Island Hotel, but others suggest it was used as a home for Mr. Rose's employees. Debris discovered during a 2012 archaeological dig, as well as a few steps beside a trail, are all that remain of the hotel today. While hiking trails, picnic tables, and the hotel and dance hall already existed, Mr. Rose added 20 cabins, a roller coaster, swimming pool, live animal exhibit, shooting gallery, carousel, and a dining hall, making it the famous summer resort we hear about today. The dance hall became a summer tradition as live music played and couples waltzed and tangoed late into the evening. The dining hall hosted the famed "Rose Island Restaurant," known to seat 500 guests at one time. With combined seating from the dance hall and an outdoor dining room, the property could accommodate over 1,600 guests. Fresh fish from the Ohio, as well as luxury items such as eggs, milk, and butter, were provided to the visiting city folks by the booming Rose Island Company. The cabins built by Mr. Rose were often rented as summer homes. Set only 100 feet from the Ohio River shoreline, they featured four rooms and fantastic views. Those well-appointed enough to afford a cabin all summer were also gifted with a free boat ride to Louisville at no charge. The zoo at Rose Island was a popular amusement, housing monkeys, raccoons, wolves, a groundhog, and a black bear named Teddy Roosevelt—named in honor of the 26th president of the United States. Remnants of the zoo are hard to find today, although parts of the metal cages remain embedded in concrete along the hillside. One of the last remaining amusements from the park is the swimming pool, which was once a remarkable sight—known throughout the Midwest as the first Olympic-sized pool in Indiana with filtered water. The pool was so well

The large, open fields at Charlestown State Park provide visitors ample opportunities for many recreational activities.

constructed, in fact, that it continued to hold water until it was deemed a safety hazard for the newly established state park.

During its height of popularity, Rose Island Amusement Park hosted 135,000 annual visitors.

Attendance declined as the Great Depression hit the area in 1929, and after decades of memories and enjoyment, Rose Island met its ultimate end with the Great Flood of 1937, which submerged the park under 10 feet of river water, causing irreparable damage. Throughout the site today, markers on signposts show the height of the floodwater. In 1940, the damaged property was purchased by INAAP. In 1963 an attempt was made to revive Rose Island by a Jefferson County judge, but the cost was too great to achieve the goal. The area lay in ruin for another 30 years before being given by INAAP for use by Charlestown State Park.

Today, a 0.9-mile loop gravel trail with guided signs leads through what remains of the once-treasured amusement park. Old, crumbling foundations where buildings once stood, the stone walkways, and the concrete swimming pool are all that remain.

FOURTEENMILE CREEK NATURE PRESERVE

In 2004, the Fourteenmile Creek Nature Preserve, which includes the Rose Island site, was dedicated and began protecting roughly 743 acres within the boundaries of Charlestown State Park. This preserve contains a dissected landscape comprising deep ravines and sinkholes on relatively level uplands with tributaries to Fourteenmile Creek and frontage on the Ohio River. High-quality natural communities found here include limestone glades, caves, and mesic upland forest. A number of very rare plants and cave invertebrates have been documented.

AMENITIES

A modern campground opened in 1997–98 and was expanded in 1999–01 to comprise 60 full hookup campsites and 132 sites with just electric. While completely surrounded by trees, the campground is wide open and flat with trees strategically placed near some of the sites. The campground facilities include flush toilets, hot water, showers, a dump station, and a water filling station. Two playgrounds exist within the park, one at the campground and another nearby between the Oak Shelter and Clark Shelter in close proximity to Trail 2.

If hiking over rough terrain along the Ohio River sounds like a good day, Charlestown State Park offers seven hiking trails, three of which are

Celandine poppies thrive in the shaded woodlands at Charlestown State Park.

rated as rugged. Because the park is situated on and among bluffs and cliffs along the river, the hiking experience is unique, with the park's main ridgeline towering hundreds of feet above the river. All of the paths are loops, with one or two lead-in tracks that travel through areas of mature forest and down through a floodplain environment.

TRAIL 1

(2.4 miles) Rugged—Beginning at the parking area, the path follows an old roadbed for a short distance before turning left and descending into the Fourteenmile Creek Valley. The trail then passes through a heavily wooded floodplain before climbing out of the valley, winding along rock outcrops, and returning to the parking area.

TRAIL 2

(1.4 miles) Moderate—The path follows several ravines, making a loop from the parking area and back. The middle section of the trail offers visitors a view of several small cascading waterfalls and flowing streams.

TRAIL 3

(2.1 miles) Rugged—The trail follows a paved path, winding to the bottom of a steep hill that originally led to a footbridge giving access to the once famed Rose Island.

TRAIL 4

(2.9 miles) Rugged—Beginning at the same parking area as Trail 3, the path follows a gentle rolling course before quickly descending downhill following the tributary streams that flow into Fourteenmile Creek. Near a halfway point of the trail, a bluff overlook gives visitors a view of the creek below from over 100 feet above the valley. The hard-packed dirt path includes a few well-placed wooden bridges that cross over seasonal streams. Although rated as rugged, there are no steep climbs.

TRAIL 5

(1.2 miles) Moderate—The trail begins near Campsite 17 in the park's campground. The path descends into a wooded ravine, leading to a platform that overlooks Fourteenmile Creek. The trail then leads back uphill, ending back at the campground. The trail can also be accessed from an overflow parking area, following the 0.3-mile spur trail outside of the campground that leads to the trail's main loop.

TRAIL 6

(2.3 miles) Rugged—The trail begins across the road from the Riverside Overlook and leads along the edge of a river bluff, giving visitors decent views of the Ohio River. The path then leads across a bridge and passes a waterfall before descending into the old Charlestown Landing site, historically used to ship and receive goods by boat. The path then continues along the bottomlands and returns near the Charlestown Land and Parking Area.

TRAIL 7

(0.9 miles) Easy—This paved path comes to the historic Portersville Bridge, which crosses Fourteenmile Creek, and into the old site of Rose Island. From here gravel paths lead a tour through the Rose Island property, returning back to the Portersville Bridge.

22

Fort Harrison State Park

Established 1996—1,700 acres

6000 N. Post Road

Indianapolis, IN 46216

(317) 591-0904

39.866667, -86.016667

One of the first settlers to the area was Elisha Reddick, who filed a claim for 132 acres and set up a homestead in October 1823. Two years later another settler named John Johnson built the area's first sawmill and gristmill along Falls Creek, making the area viable for settlement to other property owners. While the area progressed with new and surrounding development, the Reddick family lived on the property and continued to farm the land until 1903, when the property was sold to build Fort Harrison. The Reddick property was one of over 17 parcels purchased to create the park boundary we see today.

As the last forested corner left in Marion County, Fort Harrison State Park consists of 1,700-acres with two National Historic Districts. The park is named for President Benjamin Harrison to honor the man and the strong military presence that began on June 28, 1904—when the War Department issued General Order No. 117, officially announcing the purchase of land for military purposes. In 1906, President Theodore Roosevelt officially dedicated Fort Benjamin Harrison in honor of the twenty-third president and Indianapolis resident.

When the United States declared war on Germany on April 6, 1917, the military base was designated a mobilization site for the war, and

Camp Glenn was a self-contained military establishment within Fort Harrison.

men began to flood into Fort Harrison. In the passing years, the primary mission of Fort Harrison was to train young men to serve in the US Army. Douglas MacArthur and George Marshall began a model training program in 1921, and Fort Harrison hosted its first camp in 1925. The camp was named in honor of the former post commander, Colonel Edwin F. Glenn, nicknamed "the Strenuous Glenn." His biggest challenge during the early stages of operating the base was building enough housing for the large numbers of soldiers housed on the property. While some of the soldiers were sleeping in barns or on haystacks, Col. Glenn moved forward with building construction without direct permission from Washington, in order to keep his men from having to stay out in the cold and rain. Camp Edwin F. Glenn was designed to house 3,450 cadets for two camps, one in July and a second camp in August. Three hundred sixty cement slabs were poured as foundations for the camp's tent floors, with each canvas tent housing six young men. Completely self-sufficient, the camp contained 10 mess halls, five lavatories, six brick warehouses, a camp exchange store, an infirmary, and a headquarters building.

The Citizens Military Training Camp (CMTC) operated in Camp Edwin F. Glenn between 1925 and 1940, preparing volunteers for work in the Officer Reserve Corps. The CMTC was moderately self-sufficient, with facilities that included meat and vegetable storage, a motor pool, a horse transport veterinary clinic, and a medical clinic. Recreational features were provided, including a boxing ring and a swimming pool. One of the main goals of the camp was to develop leadership skills and physically train young men ages 17 to 24 with a month of military training, athletic activities, and religious education. After completing four summer camps, the men were then eligible to be hired as reserve officers. While attending the camp, young men were given free transportation, uniforms, and shoes, and they were provided with laundry services and fed every meal. Such a deal was popular during the Depression era when a mass majority of people were poor and without most of the necessities of life. Fifty thousand applied for the opportunity each year with only 35,000 chosen to enroll.

With the development of the Civilian Conservation Corps (CCC), many graduates of the camp were assigned to new camps to work for the CCC. Indiana's CCC district headquarters was established at Fort Benjamin Harrison in June 1933, providing administrative and planning support to other CCC camps located throughout the state. Fort Harrison maintained CCC camps until 1938, which included Company 3550, credited with building the original Officers Golf Club House. The last CCC recruits arrived at Fort Harrison to help build the Billings General Hospital.

In 1941, the mission of the camp changed, with the nation becoming involved in World War II. With the United States again at war, Fort Harrison was alive with activity in the war effort. Fort Harrison became the largest facility for admitting soldiers into the US Army, with 43 barracks. Aside from basic military training, the base also offered Army Finance School for those that would handle military finances, as well as Bakers and Cooks School for enlistees to learn garrison cooking and mess hall management. The Military Police School was established and operated until 1943, training military police to guard military facilities, enforce proper behavior to service personnel, and process prisoners of war. During the era of the military school, the mess halls were converted into barracks and classrooms, and the camp exchange building was doubled in size. An amphitheater was also constructed to host USO shows as entertainment for military recruits. The mission of the camp to train military police for processing prisoners of war eventually led to the camp becoming a prisoner of war camp between 1944 and 1945.

As old CCC camps were left empty, it became common practice by the nation to use these old camps to house prisoners of war. Italian POWs arrived at the camp in January of 1944 and were housed in the former CCC structures before being transferred to Ohio. In May of the same year, 300 German soldiers were transferred to the camp and placed in the old mess halls. In order to contain the prisoners, a fence was constructed around the barracks, and two guard towers were constructed. While held at the camp, prisoners were used for general labor, and the German prisoners particularly are given credit for constructing the building that would one day become the Garrison Restaurant. With new regulations on prisons instated, the prisoner of war camp at Camp Glenn was officially closed in February 1945. While most of the camps similar to the one at Fort Harrison were dismantled following the war, the brick buildings are among the few remaining military and CCC camp structures still in existence.

With the camp no longer in use, several administrative functions and training programs found a home at Fort Harrison. The Vietnam era brought a new purpose to the military base under the Vietnam Clemency Program, initiated by President Ford and President Carter in the 1970s. Both the Vietnam Joint Clemency Processing Center and the Deserter Returnee Program were located at Fort Harrison in 1974 and 1977. The program granted clemency to both deserters and draft evaders, and Fort Harrison was used to process several thousands of men from all over the world. At its peak, the military base processed 180 people a day who had deserted the Vietnam War, with an estimated 6,300 individuals entered into the program and discharged from military service.

Representing the first known effort by a state to create a national army out of a collection of state militias, the historic location served multiple roles as a troop reception center, classroom, and soldier support facility during all major military conflicts from WWI to Desert Storm. The military base's last operation in 1990 hosted soldiers with Operation Desert Shield to be deployed from Fort Harrison to the Persian Gulf. In 1991, the military management of Fort Harrison was decommissioned after the nation's defense budget was reduced, leading to the closure of US military bases throughout the world. In 1992, a group of local citizens moved to protect a 1,100-acre portion of natural landscape connected to Fort Harrison. This section represented the largest unbroken parcel of forested property in central Indiana. Embracing the idea to save the forest from development, Governor Evan Bayh worked to convert the property into a state park. Due to the land's proximity to Indianapolis, saving the property ensured that what forests were left around the city would remain for future generations.

In 1995 after years of work, 1,700 of the original 2,500 acres were deeded to the state park system by the Department of Interior for use as a recreational facility. That same year, Camp Edwin F. Glenn was designated a National Historic District to preserve the buildings and grounds.

The new park officially opened its gates with a new mission in 1996—to provide the public a natural area for recreation as well as to offer the old camp as an educational experience. The visitors' center displays a wide array of information and historical artifacts from the CMTC known as Camp Glenn, a CCC headquarters, and the World War II prisoner of war camp.

SADDLE BARN

When soldiers first arrived at Fort Harrison in 1908, they depended on horses and mules to carry people and equipment. Large stables were constructed to accommodate the animals and the operations surrounding the horses at Fort Harrison. By 1938, Fort Harrison still held 150 horses and mules for ceremonial purposes and as work animals. Since roads have been an evolving feature in American culture, horses have

The Fort Golf Resort connected to Fort Harrison State Park offers visitors an 18-hole course and a driving range.

A museum and visitors' center with military memorabilia helps to educate the public about Fort Harrison State Park's military history.

continued to be used where rough terrain prevented motorized travel. By the end of World War I, however, horses had primarily been phased out for military purposes. Today, Fort Harrison still offers a saddle barn, located within close proximity to Camp Glenn where it has always been.

GOLF COURSE

The park overlooks an 18-hole golf course designed by legendary golf architect Pete Dye with lodging within 100 yards of the course.

LODGING

Lodging options include fully furnished three-bedroom homes known as the Officers Homes, comfortable overnight suites at the Harrison House, and 27 rooms in the main lodge.

MUSEUM OF 20TH CENTURY WARFARE

Founded in August of 2004, the Museum of 20th Century Warfare is a volunteer-based museum presenting exhibits about the lives, history, artifacts, and uniforms of soldiers in World War I, World War II, the Korean War, Vietnam, and other more recent wars during the twentieth century. A 14-foot model of the USS *Indianapolis* is one of many items on permanent display, and the museum changes its temporary displays every three months, often celebrating the time period in which a specific event occurred. Volunteers with the museum also take part in reenactments and living history camps, dressing in uniforms from past wars. The museum is dedicated to its four cornerstones—education, honor, integrity, and charity—in an effort to ensure that soldiers and the wars in which they fought are never forgotten.

THE WALNUT PLANTATION

The Harrison Trace Trail that passes through the walnut plantation is part of the Indy Birding Trail. The unique walnut plantation provides a habitat for nesting Baltimore and orchard orioles, indigo buntings, cerulean warblers, brown creepers, and many other local bird species.

DOG PARK

Fort Harrison State Park offers an extensive dog park for a yearly fee and is divided into three different sections—Platoon Run (3.6 acres), Herrin Hill (1.3 acres), and Brigade Landing (5 acres). Dog park accommodations include water stations, benches, and waste stations with bags in all three sections, as well as a pond with a wooded adventure area within the Brigade Landing area. The names "Brigade" and "Platoon" were given to the dog park areas in honor of the state park's military history, while "Herrin" refers to the Herrin family who first settled in the area. Located in the northern tip of park property, it is only accessed from Fall Creek Road and cannot be accessed while inside Fort Harrison State Park. A pass is required and can be purchased at the park's visitors' center.

CHINQUAPIN NATURE PRESERVE

Located in the northeast corner, this 119.93-acre tract protects the stream corridor of the Fall Creek Valley and an important block of forested habitat in Indiana's Central Till Plain. The property's topography consists of heavily dissected slopes and ravine forests along with the floodplains of Fall Creek and its confluence with Indian Creek. The diverse ecosystem that exists contains an abundant array of flora and fauna that are area-sensitive forest interior plants and animals dependent upon large, unbroken forest ecosystems. This preserve has a high conservation value as a nesting site and contains a heron rookery, as well as a stretch of Fall Creek that is home to several species of mussels.

WARBLER WOODS NATURE PRESERVE

Located in the northeastern section of the park, the 136-acre preserve has 0.6 miles of frontage along Fall Creek and is highly dissected with gentle slopes and marsh-like forests. The preserved tract has a high-quality herbaceous layer with spring ephemerals, and the site is utilized as nesting habitat by migrant birds, including the cerulean warbler and brown creeper.

BLUFFS OF FALL CREEK NATURE PRESERVE

Located along the northwestern edge of the park, the 135-acre preserve consists of heavily dissected slopes and ravines, as well as a floodplain forest along Fall Creek at its confluence with Mud Creek. The abundance of water and forested shelter provides nesting habitat for a number of migrant birds, including the hooded warbler.

LAWRENCE CREEK NATURE PRESERVE

Located in the southwest corner of the park, the 232-acre preserve protects the Lawrence Creek drainage, an important part of the Fall Creek watershed, along with a block of forested habitat in Indiana's Central Till Plain. It consists of heavily dissected slopes with ravine forests along the botanically rich Lawrence Creek drainage, with a small area of till plain flatwoods within the unit along with their expected component flora and fauna. The site is utilized as nesting habitat for a suite of migrant birds, including the hooded warbler, brown creeper, wood thrush, ovenbird, Acadian flycatcher, and Kentucky warbler.

There are six hiking and multiuse trails at the park totaling 10 miles. Multiuse trails are heavily used by mountain bikes and are a part of the Hoosier Mountain Biking Association's list of trails. There is one horse trail that connects to the park's saddle barn and loops through the park's southwestern section. While there are no camping or overnight accommodations inside Fort Harrison State Park, the Millennium Grove Picnic Area offers visitors 27 paved spaces, each with a charcoal grill located near the park's visitors' center, the Museum of 20th Century Warfare, and the saddle barns. Unlike most other Indiana State Parks, Fort Harrison is only open during the day.

Delaware Lake at Fort Harrison State Park.

HARRISON TRACE TRAIL

(2.75 miles) Easy—This asphalt surface trail was designed for use by walkers, runners, and bicyclists, and it stretches from the western border of the park to the eastern section, making a loop around Delaware Lake and Duck Pond. Several access points exist along the path, including the Walnut Trailhead in the western section of the park and all of the park's five shelters. The eastern section of the trail creates a large loop, traveling through the Warbler Woods Nature Preserve. While the path is paved, it is not flat, and it follows the rolling uplands above Fall Creek while winding through many tree-covered and shaded environments.

LAWRENCE CREEK TRAIL—MULTIUSE

(3.6 miles) Moderate—The trail can be accessed at either the Lawrence Creek Trailhead or the Walnut Trailhead and travels across upland forests and steep ravines. While the northern section of the trail tends to remain wet all summer, the entire trail is within the boundary of the Lawrence Creek Nature Preserve where many native and rare wildflowers exist. Due to the specific species of hardwood trees in this area, the trail is also a prime spot to catch autumn color changes. The trail is designated as multiuse and is shared with mountain bikes and trail runners.

SCHOEN CREEK—MULTIUSE

(3.0 miles) Moderate—Located in the south-central section of the park, the trail begins at the parking area near the Camp Glenn Recreation Buildings and snakes back and forth, circling the Millennium Grove Picnic Area, and then it returns back to the same parking area. The dirt path is thin in most places from the constant abrasion of bicycle tires and is designated as a multiuse trail, shared with mountain bikes and trail runners. As the second-longest path in the park, it is also the most miles to be squeezed into a small section of land, giving the trail lots of twists and turns.

FALL CREEK TRAIL—HIKING

(1.1 miles) Moderate—The trail can be accessed from the northeast corner of the Delaware Lake Picnic Area or near Duck Pond in the eastern section of the park. The path's northern section follows along the low bottomlands along Fall Creek and directly through the center of the Warbler Woods Nature Preserve with several spots of elevation change. A larger and a much smaller loop make up the path, and when in the northern area along Fall Creek, the Fall Creek Boardwalk and Observation Deck allow visitors a great view of water and shaded hardwood forest.

CAMP CREEK TRAIL—HIKING

(2.0 miles) Moderate—The trail can be accessed from many locations along the paved Harrison Trace Trail and is a nice path connecting Delaware Lake and Duck Pond. The loop path travels through the southern section of the Warbler Woods Nature Preserve, passing an old army rubble pile left from the days the property was used as a military camp. Also along the path, visitors will encounter many beautiful vistas and bluffs showcasing the attractiveness of the Camp Creek Valley.

TREE ID TRAIL

(1 mile) Easy—The Tree ID Trail offers visitors a unique learning experience in which they can view native Indiana tree species along the outer edge of the Millennium Grove Picnic Area. While following the mowed trail, each wooden post with metal sign lists the tree species' name, growth form, description of the tree's wood, uses for the specific species, common habitat, range, and any other disguising features, including bark, twig, and leaf bud descriptions.

23

O'Bannon Woods State Park

Established 2004—2,294 acres

7234 Old Forest Road SW

Corydon, IN 47112

(812) 738-8232

38.228056, -86.296111

The area's main feature has historically been Wyandotte Caves, which contains over 9.4 miles of underground caverns and one of the world's largest underground mountains. Used by prehistoric Indians for thousands of years, the caves were named after 1940 resident Native Americans of the Wyandotte Nation. Tours through the caves began around 1850 by the Rothrock family, who purchased the land to be used as a mill site in 1819. The original sawmill and gristmill were built by Henry Peter Rothrock around 1836 from native oak and poplar timbers. After the mills were damaged in the winter floods of 1897, Rothrock's descendants rebuilt the mills and support pillars using native stone in 1909, and they continued to operate until the mid-1940s.

Parcels of the property were first purchased in 1932 by the Department of Conservation, and prior to the establishment of the park, the property was originally part of the 24,000-acre Harrison-Crawford State Forest, operated by the Indiana Department of Natural Resources Division of Forestry. Since its inception as one of Indiana's largest state forest properties, it has served as a source for timber. The state purchased Wyandotte Caves and Siberts Cave in 1966, and in 1974 in response to the public desiring more recreational land, 2,294 acres containing all of

A scenic forested drive through O'Bannon Woods State Park.

the property's recreational facilities were set aside within the borders of Harrison-Crawford State Forest and operated as a state recreational area.

Formerly known as Wyandotte Woods State Recreation Area, the name was changed in 2005 to honor Governor Frank O'Bannon and his family for their generosity to the state's natural resources and history.

Today, all caves on the property are closed to provide protection from white-nose syndrome, a fungus that is killing bats in large numbers in the Northeastern United States. With the caves not currently a viable feature for guests, the attractions aboveground have been expanded and emphasized.

In 1934 the Civilian Conservation Corps (CCC) Company 517 made the park property their home and began building many of the facilities, including Shelter House 2 and the property manager's residence. The camp was also home to one of Indiana's few African American CCC companies, whose residence sat where the group campsite is today. The Indian Head logo at the park's entrance gate is a representation of a carving, located at Shelter House 2, created in 1936 by an individual of CCC Company 517. After working the forest property for three years, Company 517 left in 1937 and established a new camp near South Bend, Indiana; they were

Rolling hills and hardwoods give O'Bannon State Park a rustic and primitive feel.

replaced with CCC Company 1592 in 1941. The CCC continued to be a presence in the park, planting trees and fighting fires until the CCC was phased out during World War II.

The Hickory Hollow Nature Center has become one of the best park facilities in the state, offering outdoor educational programs at its Forest Glade and Prairie Demonstration Garden—able to accommodate over 40 people in the native flora and butterfly gardens. Spectacular displays inside include a large collection of live snake habitats offering an up-close view of 12 snake species, including a nonvenomous black rat snake; eastern hognose; bullsnake; black king snake; red, eastern, and western milk snakes; western fox snake; prairie king snake; corn snake;

and rough green snake—as well as a venomous cottonmouth, timber rattlesnake, and northern copperhead. Two large aquariums house an enormous common snapping turtle and a juvenile alligator snapping turtle. More impressive is the vast collection of over 40 preserved animals displayed on the surrounding walls, including an albino white-tailed deer, bison, elk, black bear, a fully intact fur of a timber wolf, and a large collection of winged predators and fish. Large glass cases line the walls and include a huge collection of Smokey the Bear memorabilia, including old posters, patches, stickers, pamphlets, and stuffed toys celebrating the Smokey the Bear legacy. A similar glass case includes photos and antiques from the park's African American CCC Company showcasing their work in the park as well as photos, articles, and items from the park's former employees, including the original state park uniform worn by Harrison-Crawford's foreman Lafe C. Cline while employed between 1932 and 1942. Two diaries from forest engineer Dewey N. Hickman are on display, which are said to include the original written notes on many land acquisitions for Harrison-Crawford and many other Department of Natural Resource properties. Two large wooden-tiered floor displays showcase fossils, arrowheads, primitive tools, and gemstones dating back to prehistoric Middle Archaic, Paleo-Indian, and Early Woodland eras. A separate bird-viewing room offers visitors an opportunity to watch wildlife through its one-way glass window in a room that is decorated with a display of bird feathers and hundreds of preserved moths, butterflies, bugs, beetles, and other creepy crawlers common to the local area.

The inside of the nature center is just the beginning, as the back door leads out to a man-made wetland garden with water-loving plants, frogs, turtles, and fish, and sidewalks lined with beautiful native flora. The path leads directly to a historic barn restored to its 1850s condition, housing the fully operational Leavenworth-Lang-Cole hay press and accompanying exhibits of vintage clothing and tools from the time period. The restored hay press is one of several hundred that once operated in the Ohio River Valley around the 1800s and is built into the barn's structure, standing about 35 feet high and weighing around five tons. The press was originally located around five miles away from where it sits today, along the Blue River near Leavenworth, and was built by Zebulon Leavenworth, later owned by the Langs, and donated to the Indiana Department of Natural Resources by Dr. Jack Cole and his family. While six hay presses once existed in the Harrison-Crawford area, today only about a dozen or so are known to exist in all of the United States.

An antique hay press, built around the 1850s, still operates today for special events.

Behind the barn is a pioneer farmstead constructed by volunteers and the park's staff starting in 1980—originally envisioned by park employee Merle Behr, who designed the farmstead to be used for living-history demonstrations. The farmstead is representative of a typical homestead in the 1830s and includes a working blacksmith forge and pioneer herb garden as well as many other vintage services. Volunteers and staff continue to host the buildings on certain days of the year, dressed in authentic attire while demonstrating work and life as it would have been during the time period.

MOUTH OF BLUE RIVER NATURE PRESERVE

Located in the southwestern section of the park, the 470-acre preserve's topography consists of several knobs, deep ravines, and steep bluffs. Due in part to the varied topography in this preserve, there are several high-quality natural communities and associated rare plant and animal species.

POST OAK/CEDAR NATURE PRESERVE

Established to preserve the land in a natural state, the 266-acre preserve is open for walking only along an interesting trail with contrasting habitats. Heavily shaded by cedars near the entrance and parking area, the trail abounds with ferns and colored mosses before soon turning sunny, dry, and rocky with an abundance of sun-loving wildflowers such as twinleaf and hoary puccoon lining the path's edges. While located along the edge of O'Bannon Woods State Park, the Post Oak-Cedar Nature Preserve is not within the park's borders and remains its own property.

AMENETIES

The nature center offers a small display covering the fire tower that was first built in 1932, including the tower's original Osborne Fire Finder, used to provide accurate and precise directional information on the distance and location of a fire from the fire tower. At one time dozens of towers existed throughout Indiana, each one working with the others to triangulate the location of a forest fire. Made of wood, the original fire tower had to be replaced with an updated steel-frame tower in 1941, which still exists today. One hundred thirty-four steps take visitors to the top of the 90-foot tower, where they can enjoy a panoramic view of southern Indiana's skyline above the forest canopy.

To replace a long-closed swimming pool, the park built a new family aquatic center in 2007. The park offers 281 campsites with electric, 47 nonelectric horseman/primitive sites, and a group camping structure.

Eight hiking trails sprawl through O'Bannon Woods, offering dozens of miles to explore the heavily wooded forest, often sharing or crossing paths with bike and horse trails.

FIRE TOWER TO ROCKY RIDGE HIKE AND BIKE TRAIL

(2 miles) Moderate to Rugged—The trail begins at the fire tower and travels west, intersecting with the Rocky Ridge Trail. Combined with

A bird's-eye view of the lush forest that encompasses Harrison-Crawford State Forest and O'Bannon Woods and the Blue River that winds its way through the property.

the Rocky Ridge Trail and with a return to the Fire Tower Trail, this route provides six miles of mountain biking and hiking trail. Parking, a comfort station, and water are available at the fire tower.

ROCKY RIDGE HIKE AND BIKE TRAIL

(2 miles) Moderate—This trail begins and ends near campsite 35. The trail loop passes through deep ravines and up scenic, rocky slopes. Parking and water are available at the campground.

TULIP VALLEY TRAIL

(1 mile) Moderate—A gravel path leading into the forest away from the pioneer farmstead begins the Tulip Valley Universally Accessible Resource Trail, designed to take visitors into a unique and educational woodland experience. The approximately one-mile trail loops through the forest passing mysterious holes, a long list of tagged tree species, and an opportunity to view birds and wildlife at a wildlife viewing station. The trail loops to the west, ending at the nature center parking lot. The Tulip Valley Trail was made possible by a cooperative of community organizations and partnerships that raised or donated the funds needed to create a premier educational outdoor experience everyone can enjoy; the trail is laid with seven million pounds of gravel to ensure a smooth and enjoyable walk through the woods.

CCC GHOST TRAIL

(1.5 miles) Rugged—The loop trail begins and ends near the group camp where the original 1930s CCC camp once existed. The rocky and moderately steep terrain make the trail a haven for dozens of wildflowers and ferns, and the trail travels over exposed, mossy rocks and through dry creek beds. If rain is persistent, the creek will hold water.

CLIFF DWELLER TRAIL

(1.75 miles) Moderate—This loop trail crosses a dry creek bed, follows a beautiful, spring-fed creek, and has some long stretches of steep climbing. Parking is available at the Pioneer Cabin Shelter House.

WHITE-TAILED DEER TRAIL

(0.9 miles) Easy—The trail begins in the parking area near Shelter House 2 Picnic Area and sprawls through open woodlands and large patches of mayapples. The trail offers a quiet retreat away from busy roads and down a few steep hills before ending at the road that leads to Shelter House 2 parking.

OHIO RIVER BLUFF TRAIL

(1.5 miles) Rugged—Located at the end of the parking lot for the Ohio River Picnic Area, the trail travels a flat pathway just feet away from the edge of the Ohio River before turning to lead up a steep, rocky hill. Along the rocky path, the trail is scattered with wildflowers, especially large patches of shooting stars along the trail's edges. Upon reaching the top of the hill, the trail opens into the grassy field of Shelter House 2. Crossing the field, the trail picks back up, heading back into the woods and immediately downhill for approximately 0.18 miles over stone steps built by the CCC, before ending at the road leading to the Ohio River Picnic Area.

POST OAK-CEDAR NATURE PRESERVE TRAIL

(0.8 miles) Rugged—The trail is named for the two most common trees found in the area, post oak and eastern red cedar. The trail offers 25 educational trail stations numbered with wooden posts, identifying trees, natural grass patches, shrubs, and ferns; it is best experienced by using one of the free, illustrated brochures explaining what can be seen at each station.

UNIVERSALLY ACCESSIBLE RESOURCE LOOP TRAIL

(1 mile) Easy—A one-of-a-kind trail in the Indiana State Park System, the Universally Accessible Trail allows access to anyone who is interested in exploring nature, no matter what. With a grade elevation of only five percent, the trail is designed to be used at a relaxed speed. Thanks to funding from the Harrison County Community Foundation and an Access to Recreation Grant from the Kellogg's cereal corporation, a six-foot-wide path was constructed through a heavily wooded section of the park. Located directly behind the nature center, the trail is tailored for individuals who require a smoother grade or are in a wheelchair. The trail is fully accessible, with educational signs about wildlife and trees scattered along the route. For those who need extra assistance, the nature center even offers a collection of all-terrain wheelchairs, four-wheel drive electric chairs, and a golf cart.

24

Prophetstown State Park

Established 2004—2,000 acres

5545 Swisher Road

West Lafayette, IN 47906

(765) 567-4919

40.5, -86.833333

The landscape where Prophetstown State Park resides was once carved out by the rushing meltwaters of prehistoric glaciers, creating river valleys and a terraced landscape. Not long after the glaciers receded, Native people began to arrive to the area and thrived within the prairie countryside.

The idea for a park first began from a failed attempt to create some form of recreational area near the Lafayette region starting in the 1960s. By 1992, the state bought a 10-acre parcel with a small fishing pond known as the Kline property. The state later purchased 300 acres known as the Yost property, which is used today as the park's 1920s-era farm.

The first surveys of the area noted a distinct division between two ecosystems, with prairies covering the west part of the state and thick forest stretching all the way to the east. This division created a unique ecosystem known as a prairie savanna, defined with diverse fields of prairie understory and a patchwork of large trees. Today the area is constantly being restored to its presettlement conditions, including a restored prairie with native species and rare wetland ecosystems known as fens. Characterized by the growth of grasses, sedges, and wildflowers,

The 1920s-era farm at Prophetstown State Park.

fens are created when groundwater rich in calcium seeps from a slope and runs downhill. Having percolated through limestone, the groundwater of the fen is alkaline, while swamps are normally acidic. This unique detail allows rare species of plants, such as queen of the prairie, bottle gentian, turtlehead, and swamp betony, to be found at Prophetstown State Park. Because prairie wetlands were farmed extensively, causing a great deal of ecological damage, few large expanses still exist today. Prophetstown State Park has made it their main goal to change that by restoring over 1,500 acres of prairie.

Glacial stone is an ever-present theme to the park, with its bridges lined with metamorphic and igneous rock deposited by glaciers that originated in Canada. After receding, these glaciers left sand, gravel, and boulders forming 450 feet of glacial till. The stones from these deposits were often removed by farmers when the land was first used for agriculture. Today, these same stones are used for decorative purposes throughout the park, as a means of representing the area's rich, geological history.

A gorgeous sunrise at Prophetstown State Park floods the native prairies with colorful hues.

The park's concrete bridge, for example, is covered with such glacial stones, known as erratics, acquired from the former Vulcan Materials sand and gravel pit located adjacent to the park's property.

While the area was once heavily used for farming, the park currently preserves 2,000 acres of prairie, forest, wetlands, and savannas. The layout of the park is in a three-terrace formation with the first terrace located in a floodplain by the Wabash River, the second 15 to 40 feet above the floodplain, and the third terrace marking the highest point of the park. Originally proposed in 1989, fundraising between 1994 and 1999 helped the idea of the park eventually come to fruition in 2004.

Indiana's newest state park is named in honor of a Native American village that was established by Tecumseh in 1808 between the rivers. Tenskwatawa, known as the Prophet, was a religious leader, and along with his brother, Tecumseh, a military and political leader, they were able to assemble over a thousand Native people from 14 different tribes to push back against the westward expansion of European settlers. The village was the main stage for Tecumseh's legendary brother to speak, named by the people as the Prophet. Choosing to strike first in the early morning hours, the massive Native American army attacked 1,200 of Governor William Henry Harrison's troops before withdrawing into the marshlands two hours later. The feud resulted in Harrison's men burning

Wild bergamot highlight a field that surrounds the Native American village at Prophetstown State Park.

Prophetstown to the ground. When Tecumseh later returned to find the confederation destroyed, he sided with the British in the War of 1812, hoping to defeat the Americans who were taking over his peoples' land through brute force. While Tecumseh later died in 1813 near present-day Detroit, the tribes that remained in Indiana—the Miami (whose land this originally was), the Powatomi, and others—were all eventually removed by force, after inhabiting the land for thousands of years.

With the end of the War of 1812, settlers flooded the area from Ohio, leading to Indiana's population increasing by 455 percent in just 10 years. One of the first settlers to establish a home and business in the area was William Burnett. A French fur trader, Burnett established a trading post with his wife Kaudema, the daughter of a Potawatomi chief. The influx of trade to the area created a nearby township in Battleground, Indiana, and one of the first white settlers known to build a log cabin was Henry Davis in 1823. During this era, trade routes were deemed the only viable source of income, since the wetlands that sprawled throughout the landscape were perceived to be unusable for farming because they would not grow trees. It wasn't until John Deere invented a plow in 1840 that could break through the wetland prairie's incredible root system that people quickly realized that the area's soil was some of the most nutrient-rich soil in the world. Once thought to cause illness due to the moisture-rich air, the wetlands were drained of their water using steam-powered dredges, and clay tiles were used to continually drain the fields.

A 1.49-mile road extension entering into Prophetstown State Park was completed and dedicated on June 9, 2016.

NATIVE AMERICAN VILLAGE

The original Prophetstown was the capital of a Native American confederacy from 1809 until 1811. It seems only fitting that the park would highlight the people of Prophetstown and their efforts with a replica of a Woodland Indian Settlement. This open-air museum features reproductions of a traditional medicine lodge, chief's cabin, council house, granary, shade shelter, cooking hearth, double-conical home, and wigwam.

THE VISITORS' CENTER AND GREENHOUSES

Plants used to restore the property back to presettlement conditions are grown by the park's staff in greenhouses. They grow tens of thousands of wildflowers and grasses every year—mostly for restoration

A handmade wigwam sits within the Native American village at Prophetstown State Park.

purposes—but a small fraction are sold to the public to encourage the use of native plants in their own landscaping.

THE FARM AT PROPHETSTOWN

A 1920s farmstead highlights sustainable agriculture, homesteading, and heirloom gardening—with a unique experience of all aspects of early farm life. Operating on a 94.5-acre property leased by Prophetstown State Park, the farm operates as a nonprofit organization teaching visitors about historical agriculture and the homesteading arts.

The Gibson Farmhouse

A larger replica of another farmhouse used during the 1920s is a reproduction of the "Hillrose" kit house that could originally have been purchased in 1918 from the Sears, Roebuck & Company catalog. Known as the Gibson Farmhouse, a structure such as this would have been ordered by mail and delivered by rail, costing only $6,880, with labor included, to construct. The replica that is used today for the farmstead's main farmhouse cost considerably more.

Hampton House

One of the farm's authentic Sears & Roebuck farmhouses was moved to the site in 2004.

While farm animals of all sorts are scattered throughout the farm, other buildings on the property include a smokehouse, machine shed, Model-T garage, Model-A garage, chicken coop—which can house 50 hens—several authentic barns, and a blacksmith shop.

CAMPGROUNDS

The park campground offers 55 sites with full hookups and an additional 55 with only electric. The facilities include a modern shower and restroom building, as well as playgrounds.

AQUATIC CENTER

An aquatic center is a popular feature of the park, with a 30-foot tube slide, body flume, lazy river float area, adventure channel, zero-entry pool, and an aquatic activity center for water sports. Able to accommodate 700 people, the enormous facility also includes showers, a changing area, restrooms, and a concession area. One of the most attractive buildings in the park, the facility was designed to blend into the park's natural landscape. Outside the facility, native grasses and wildflowers

Native grasses like Indian Grass encompass the fields that have been restored to presettlement conditions.

are strategically planted to help re-create the feel of a native prairie land-scape, all while relaxing amid the state's only outdoor facility to have such a wide array of features similar to a full-scale water park.

NATURALIST SERVICES

Naturalists lead an abundance of interpretive programs, and many seasonal events are scheduled year-round. Prophetstown State Park is a long, rolling landscape with over 11 miles of hiking trails, including wide, paved, accessible paths that flow through the native park prairies.

VILLAGE TRAIL

(2.8 miles) Easy—This trail connects the Native American village to the farm and winds around the prairie to include a new section through an oak savannah.

TRAIL 1

(2.25 miles) Easy—The loop trail begins and ends at the Meadow View parking area, winding through a former Christmas tree plantation of Douglas fir before reaching the Prairie View Group picnic area. The trail continues into a fen and leads through a marshy area, before entering a field of wild cherry and mulberry.

TRAIL 2

(1.9 miles) Moderate—North of the Blazingstar Picnic Area, the trail begins on Trail 1, following a shaded path running along the edge of Harrison Creek. In the spring, the wildflowers in this woodland section are amazing. The trail leads through a mature sycamore grove before merging back with Trail 1 just north of the campground.

TRAIL 3

(3.5 miles) Moderate—Near the east end of the pond, the trail leads off of Trail 2, following a gravel road. Near the point where the Wabash and Tippecanoe Rivers meet, the trail turns into a dirt path. The trail then leads through large-scale prairie restoration areas, across wet bottom-lands, and onto spectacular overlooks that allow visitors to observe the park's stunning collection of fens. The trail ends near its starting point, uphill and north of the pond.

TRAIL 4

(2.1 miles) Easy—The trail begins along Trail 3, near the Tippecanoe River. The path leads through a heavily shaded forest in a floodplain. The trail leads along a one-way path to the most northeastern section of park property, returning back along the same route.

PAVED HIKE/BIKE PATH

(5 miles) Easy—The paved path leads visitors through every feature the park offers, heading from west to east. Starting near the park's gate-house, the trail ends at the Tippecanoe River. Traveling through the majority of the park's meadows, the bike path is a great way to experience the beautiful array of prairie ecosystems that exist along the way.

NATHAN D. STRANGE is a writer, naturalist, and author of *A Guide to the Knobstone Trail*.

MATT WILLIAMS has worked for the Nature Conservancy for the past 16 years and is a specialist in prescribed fire and endangered species management. He is author and photographer of *Indiana State Parks: A Centennial Celebration*.